SAFE

MONEY

IN
TOUGH
TIMES

QUANTITY SALES

Most Dell books are available at special quantity discounts when purchased in bulk by corporations, organizations, and special-interest groups. Custom imprinting or excerpting can also be done to fit special needs. For details write: Dell Publishing, 666 Fifth Avenue, New York, NY 10103. Attn.: Special Sales Department.

INDIVIDUAL SALES

Are there any Dell books you want but cannot find in your local stores? If so, you can order them directly from us. You can get any Dell book in print. Simply include the book's title, author, and ISBN number if you have it, along with a check or money order (no cash can be accepted) for the full retail price plus $2.00 to cover shipping and handling. Mail to: Dell Readers Service, P.O. Box 5057, Des Plaines, IL 60017.

SAFE

MONEY

IN
TOUGH TIMES

**A Step-by-Step Action Plan
to Protect You and Your Family
in 1991**

Jonathan Pond

A DELL BOOK

Published by
Dell Publishing
a division of
Bantam Doubleday Dell Publishing Group, Inc.
666 Fifth Avenue
New York, New York 10103

ISBN: 0-440-21085-2

Printed in the United States of America

Published simultaneously in Canada

January 1991

10 9 8 7 6 5 4 3 2 1

RAD

CONTENTS

PART III

INVESTING IN TOUGH ECONOMIC TIMES

PART IV

TACKLING SPECIAL SITUATIONS

PART V

PLANNING FOR A SECURE FINANCIAL FUTURE

Acknowledgments

Several very capable people assisted me in the preparation of this book. Viveca Gardiner was instrumental in all phases. Jody Rein, my editor at Dell, offered round-the-clock support, as well as many excellent comments that have improved the book immensely. Cindy Andrade ably assisted us in the copyediting chores, and Kolette Brown and Kerry Doherty were very helpful in the preparation of the manuscript. I sincerely appreciate the efforts of all of you.

Introduction

In spite of how helpless you feel riding the economic rollercoaster, there is a way for you to overcome the fear and confusion of the 1991 recession. There's no more critical time than now to stop letting your finances control you so that you can control your finances. You can't rely on others to do it for you. There is a way out, and this book will help you. It will make sense out of the often conflicting and always confusing opinions of "experts" about what you should be doing with your investments and other personal financial matters during the recession. This is not a "get rich quick" book; perhaps it could be called a "get rich sensibly" book. Unlike other authors who have published books in past recessions, I will not tell you to put all of your money into gold or canned goods or to hide your money in a cave or ship it overseas. I'm also not predicting a depression, but I think we could be in for a formidable and lengthy recession.

If you're looking for something bizarre to do with your money, you've come to the wrong book. Money is too hard earned to waste on some incredibly inappropriate investment. What I will show you, however, is how to invest wisely and well during a recession, using investments that you already understand. But there is a lot more involved in surviving this recession than investing. I will help you if and when you become a victim of the slow economy—if you lose your job or fear that you may lose your job, if you get into debt problems, or if you're having trouble affording college tuition for your children. An entire section of the book, entitled "Tackling Special Situations" addresses the problems that will befall many people in 1991.

Recessions need not be totally negative experiences, however. Because our financial lives are at least a little unsettled during an uncertain economy, we are forced to take a closer look at the way we manage and spend our money. 1991 will not be a bad year to begin to discard some bad financial habits and replace them with better habits. Believe it or not, there are many opportunities to grow financially during a recession, and these opportunities will be discussed in the chapters that follow. I hope you will use this book in good health . . . and good wealth.

P A R T

I

UNDERSTANDING THE RECESSION

1

WHAT'S GOING ON IN THE ECONOMY?

What's going to happen to me?

There's no doubt about it: 1991 is going to be a tough year for Americans. This book will help you and your family survive it. Whatever problems the bad economy dishes out to you, you will find help in these pages. How bad are things out there? In just one day in late 1990 the following events happened:

- Stocks and bonds both weakened significantly.
- Ford increased its loan loss reserves at its big S&L subsidiary.
- General Motors announced that it was going to idle at least eleven U.S. assembly plants, amid weakening sales.
- Chrysler posted a $214 million third-quarter loss.
- World petroleum prices rose.
- Airlines announced fare boosts.
- A major consulting company laid off 17 percent of its employees.
- Employee-benefits experts indicated that early-retirement incentive plans appear to be losing favor as an alternative to outright firings.

What's going on with the economy? And more importantly, what does it mean to you? How will you and your family be affected? What should you do now to protect yourself from the tough times ahead? Some people, for a variety of reasons, are severely affected by a recession. What if you're one of them? This book will help you understand what's going on, and more importantly, will show you what you can do to survive the economic downturn, no matter how badly you are affected. What's more, this book will show you ways to take control over and manage your finances in such a way that future recessions—and there will be future recessions—will be minor annoyances to you, rather than the calamities they can be for millions of Americans who are unprepared for financial adversity.

What's Going On in the Economy?

Many problems were building up in the economy long before Saddam Hussein invaded Kuwait. Since then, these problems have come to the fore. Unless you've had your head in the sand, you are painfully aware of what is going on.

- Stock prices are way down.
- Layoffs abound.
- Salaries are being frozen or cut.
- Interest rates are volatile.
- Real estate prices are declining in many areas.
- People are unable to sell their homes.
- Corporate profits are down.
- Manufacturing plants are closing, across the nation.
- Congress passed the largest single tax increase in history.
- Many real estate limited partnerships have collapsed.

- The automobile industry is suffering from slow sales.
- Retailers are on the ropes.
- Gasoline and fuel-oil costs have risen significantly.
- Families are choking on debt.
- Real estate foreclosures are rising.
- Federal, state, and local governments are posting record budget deficits.
- The trade deficit continues in spite of cheaper U.S. products overseas.
- The U.S. dollar is getting weaker and weaker.
- The junk-bond market has collapsed.
- The banking industry is in crisis.
- Taxpayers will bear the brunt of the massive S&L bailout.
- Consumer confidence is plummeting.

These problems are not going to go away very soon. A record period of prosperity has come abruptly to an end, and we're in for some tough times ahead.

What Is a Recession, and Are We Going Through One?

What is a recession? Although each recession differs in its impact, a recession is generally a period of decline: in the total output of goods and services in the country, in corporate income, in employment levels, and in foreign trade levels. Many sectors of the economy contract during a recession. Recessions reduce employment and demand for goods, so wages and corporate profits decline, thus reducing the government's tax revenue.

Are we going through a recession? The expert consensus in late 1990 is that we are either in a recession or rapidly approaching one. The economy usually sends out warning signals long in advance of a recession. Four leading economic indicators historically have been reliable in signaling an impending economic downturn.

1. **Declining stock prices.** As you probably know, stock prices declined substantially in 1990.

2. **Declining consumer confidence.** Organizations that measure consumer confidence in the economy were reporting that consumers have become very pessimistic in late 1990.

3. **Declining or flat factory orders.** New factory orders are a good measure of the health of the economy. When we are optimistic about business, we order more new parts and products from factories. Measures of factory orders in late 1990 indicated sluggish orders, thereby signaling that the overall economy was contracting.

4. **Rising unemployment claims.** The unemployment rate held relatively steady in late 1990, but at a considerably higher level than it was a year ago.

Various Recession Scenarios

How bad will this recession be? Economists are divided as to the severity of the economic downturn. As 1990 draws to a close, many observers are becoming more pessimistic about the depth of the recession. Those who earlier did not foresee a recession are becoming convinced that we are in for a very sluggish economy, if not a mild recession. Many of those who forecasted a mild recession are beginning to feel that it will be worse than they had originally expected.

At the risk of oversimplifying a very complex, unforeseeable outcome, economists tend to be divided into three different camps. The first group foresees a *sluggish economy with no recession*. Other economic forecasters predict a *mild recession* where the inflation rate will hover around 5 percent, and we could emerge from a mild recession by late 1991. Several factors could cause this mild recession scenario to unravel, notably an escalation of the Mideast crisis. Other factors, including a reduction in consumer spending (a mild recession assumes flat spending); continued high, rather than leveling, oil prices; and deepening problems in the banking industry, could bring about the third forecast, a *deep recession*. Some forecasters predict a prolonged and deep recession with double-digit unemployment and dramatic increases in bankruptcies and bank failures. One reason some economists predict this is that the recession is beginning with unprecedented high debt levels, and they fear that many companies and families will have a great deal of difficulty meeting their loan obligations. In a severe recession, interest rates could rise rather than decline as they usually do during a recession (as a result of governmental monetary policy). Unemployment could jump to 8 percent of the work force, and investor confidence would plummet. Mideast war could be a stimulus to such a gloomy scenario, particularly if oil supplies are so disrupted that oil prices soar.

Where You Live Might Affect You During the Recession

How and when you will be affected by the recession may depend on where you live. Many areas of the country already seem immersed in a recession, while others are barely on the brink. The country's major cities either are in recession as of late 1990 or headed in that direction. It is generally believed that Boston, New York, Philadelphia, Washington, and Chicago are now in a recession while Los Angeles, San Francisco, Houston, Dallas, and Detroit are headed in that direction. The following are 1991 capsule outlooks for each of the six regions of the United States.

Northeast. The heavily oil-dependent Northeast was in bad straits even before the Mideast crisis, and economists expect that it will be suffering throughout 1991. The most optimistic feel a turnaround may commence late in 1991, although by all accounts any return to prosperity is several years off. The entire region is suffering from slumping real estate prices, rising unemployment, and a weakening service sector. New England is in the worst shape in the region, and its banking industry is suffering deep problems. New York State is not far behind, with slow job growth predicted for the rest of the 1990s. The banking and brokerage industries already have reduced almost 100,000 jobs, office vacancies are rising, and New York City is experiencing tremendous fiscal problems. The only relative bright spots in the Northeast are Pennsylvania (exclusive of Philadelphia) and New Jersey, both of which enjoy diversified economies that provide varied opportunities for workers and businesses.

Midwest. In 1990, people in the Midwest probably were wondering what all the recession talk was about. The Midwest economy was still expanding, although at a slowing rate. Many economists expect the Midwest will be less affected by an economic downturn than most other regions, although a prolonged nationwide recession would certainly take its toll. One bright spot will be the farm economy, which is expected to stay strong. The region's manufacturers are heavily dependent on sales of big-ticket consumer items, such as automobiles. Until very recently, automobile sales have been stable. Thus, to a certain extent, if consumer spending for these items continues to be robust, the Midwest regional economy should continue to do well. Also, the cheap U.S. dollar will help sustain export-oriented manufacturers. On the downside,

Midwest housing construction and home prices began to weaken in 1990, which, combined with now weakening car sales, is beginning to affect the region's economy.

Northwest. The booming Northwest may be the region least affected by a nationwide recession. With the exception of a slump in the timber industry, most of this region's major industries, including high technology, aerospace, and trade with Asia, remain strong, although growth will slow or stagnate in 1991. Agriculture remains a bright spot, but the mining industry outlook is uncertain. Higher oil prices will provide a windfall for Alaska, which seems poised for a boom.

Southwest. Though there is clear evidence of a slowing of the high growth of the 1980s, the Southwest will continue to have several advantages over other regions. Forecasters see slower job growth, but no reversal, and the entertainment industry and trade with the Pacific Rim should continue to be strong. Defense is a big question mark. The defense industry was slumping until the crisis in the Gulf, and many feel that its long-term prospects remain lackluster. California's real estate market is slowing down, and elsewhere in the region, commercial real estate still hasn't recovered from its past overbuilding. Whether the strengths and past momentum in the Southwest will prevent the region as a whole from contracting in 1991 or beyond is uncertain.

Oil Patch. The Oil Patch, which includes Texas, Oklahoma, Arkansas, and Louisiana, has begun a slow recovery from the economic devastation of declining oil prices in the 1980s. High oil prices caused by the Gulf crisis have not yet had a significant effect on the skittish oil industry. Real estate continues to be a sore point, and office vacancies in the major Texas cities remain high, although they have fallen sharply since the region hit bottom. The banking industry, and soft real estate prices, continues to cause problems in the Oil Patch economy. If nothing else, this region has learned from its suffering in the 1980s and therefore has a better understanding than other regions of the country of what it takes to survive economic travails.

Southeast. The booming Southeast economy appears to be in for tough times. Unusually high growth in the late 1980s has slowed, and experts expect the economy to slip into a recession in early 1991, if it hasn't already. Their problems are similar to those experienced in other regions, most notably real estate and banking. Much of the region remains heavily dependent upon manufacturing, which, along with the service sector, will bleed during economic contraction. One plus for the region is its growing service sector, which provides it with a more balanced economy. Another plus: Atlanta will receive a boost from hosting the 1996 Olympic Games.

What a Recession Means to You. While people are affected by recessions in different ways, you can pretty much count on the following conditions in 1991.

- Inflation will slow from its temporarily high rate of about 6 percent in 1990. However, a deepening of the Mideast crisis could quickly precipitate higher inflation through dramatically higher fuel prices.

- Consumers will probably reduce their spending in 1991, and this can have a dramatic impact on many industries that depend on consumer spending. Some economists feel that the high consumer debt burden will put a significant damper on spending, while others feel that, although consumers are loaded with debt, they will continue to spend at current rates.

- Most salaries will keep pace with inflation. Nevertheless, many particularly weak sectors of the economy, like heavy industry, are likely to hold

the line on wage increases. The unemployment
rate will rise and could well add one million people
to the jobless rolls.

- Service industry employees will suffer the brunt
of this recession. The beleaguered finance, insurance, and real estate industries currently employ
nearly seven million people. White collar workers
will be laid off in great numbers in many service
industries. Construction workers, numbering five
million, are also likely to be adversely affected by
the contraction in the economy.

- Employers will convert many full-time jobs to
part-time jobs, which will open up opportunities
for part-time workers and will provide at least
some relief for unemployed full-time workers.

- The effect of a recession on your investments is
very uncertain. Most investment experts are urg-
ing investors to restrict themselves to the highest-
quality securities. The major retreat of stock
prices in 1990 certainly provides opportunities for
venturesome stock investors who look to invest
for the long term. But they must be prepared for
the possibility of further weakening of stock
prices, since given their present levels and the
dismal outlook in many industries, stocks are
hardly bargains. Quality is of particular importance for interest-earning investments. Bonds or
notes of marginal companies, companies in troubled industries, and weak municipalities should be
avoided.

Real estate, the third major investment category, is very difficult to evaluate, in part due to
wide variations in real estate prospects in various
regions of the country. Bargains can be had, but
they are a lot more difficult to find than many
investors think. The recession will continue to

result in major and widespread problems in the
real estate industry.
• Finally, when the economy recovers, the recovery
will likely be weak, and may drag on. A slow
recovery may mean that some companies and
individuals may continue to be plagued by the
economic downturn for a period of years, not
months. Many economists also feel that the recovery will be accompanied by higher inflation,
which, of course, will drive up living costs and
borrowing costs. Retirees, in particular, will be
adversely affected if inflation heats up.

A Guide for Surviving the Economic Doldrums

Now you have some understanding of the impact of
a sluggish or contracting economy in 1991 and beyond.
You should begin to consider what actions you need
to take, both to survive the downturn and to emerge
from it in sound financial condition, so that you can
take advantage of the prosperity that historically follows recessions. The next chapter provides some information on things you can do right away to minimize
the effect of the recession on your finances. The
remainder of the book is divided into four sections:
Coping with Tough Economic Times; Investing in
Tough Economic Times; Tackling Special Situations;
and Planning for a Secure Financial Future. As if it
isn't bad enough that we have to learn how to cope
with a lousy economy, our lives are further complicated by the tax law passed in late 1990, which takes
effect in 1991. The Appendix tells you how you will be
affected by the new tax rules.

Parts II and III will guide you through a variety of
concerns as you try to grapple with your personal
finances in 1991, including saving, personal debt man-

agement, budgeting, reducing expenses, insurance, and of course, investments.

After discussing recession-related problems that affect everyone, I deal in Part IV with special situations that may be of concern. In fact, it is quite likely that a few of these special situations will apply to you and your family. They include coping with unemployment, dealing with salary freezes, working through credit problems, and helping your family survive the psychological problems that often accompany distressed family finances. This section also includes tips for worried retirees, survival strategies for small business owners, and some additional guidance on two possible outcomes of the current economic malaise: a worsening recession and inflation.

The last section of the book will provide some advice to help you recover from the effects of the recession so that you can prosper in the next economic boom. When all is said and done, financial security is what personal financial planning is all about. Unfortunately, we are going through a period of time that may interrupt a lot of people's progress toward achieving financial peace of mind. I hope that after reading the pages that follow and taking appropriate action, this recession will be but a minor disruption in your personal financial progress.

2

CHECKLIST OF THINGS TO DO TODAY TO GET YOUR FINANCIAL ACT TOGETHER

I remember the recession of the early '80s. We had a real tough time—almost lost the house. We're in better financial shape now, but I still worry about what's going to happen. I want to be prepared this time.

Tough economic times affect us all; unfortunately, some people suffer more than others. Don't wait for recession problems to crop up in your personal finances. You can do a number of things today to prepare for troubles that may lie ahead. The rest of the book will describe these important matters in more depth and help you address problems that may affect you during the recession, such as investing in uncertain times, family money problems, and unemployment. The following checklist can help you begin to organize your financial life so you will not be taken by surprise if and when a financial problem arises during the recession.

Budgeting and Record Keeping

☐ Prepare a household budget that lists past and expected future income and expenses. Through the budget, you can identify spending patterns and adjust them, if necessary, to reflect changes in your financial situation or outlook. (See Chapter Five.)

☐ Evaluate your sources of income and how you spend your money so that you can plan ways to earn extra income or reduce expenses, should the need arise. (See Chapters Six and Seven.)

☐ Prepare a summary of your assets and liabilities so that you can get an idea of what you own and what you owe. This summary will help you identify what resources you have available to meet future obligations.

☐ Organize your personal records so that you have ready access to important family documents and personal financial information. If you need to address a pressing financial problem, the last thing you'll want to spend your time on is locating and organizing your records.

Insurance

You don't want to risk an expensive uninsured loss in the midst of a recession. Review your insurance policies to make sure you have adequate, but not excessive, coverage in the following areas. (See Chapter Ten.)

☐ Health insurance
☐ Homeowner's or renter's insurance
☐ Automobile insurance
☐ Extended personal liability (umbrella) insurance
☐ Disability insurance
☐ Life insurance

Debt Management

☐ Summarize your loans and other obligations, including payment schedules, so that you can plan to meet these obligations comfortably in 1991. (See Chapter Nine.)

☐ Request a credit-rating report from your local credit bureau, and review it for accuracy. (See Chapter Eight.)

☐ Review your loan status to determine your capacity to increase your borrowing if you need to during the recession.

☐ Reevaluate any major contemplated purchases, such as a home, home improvements, or an automobile, in light of the current economic situation. It may make sense to postpone these purchases.

Saving and Investing

☐ Summarize your investments so that you can:
  • Ensure they are appropriate in light of current and expected economic and market conditions. (See Chapters Thirteen, Fourteen, and Fifteen.)
  • Make sure they are properly diversified. (See Chapter Eleven.)
  • Determine which investments you could cash in easily to meet emergency financial needs, if necessary.

☐ Determine whether you have sufficient ready resources to meet three to six months' living expenses in the event of a financial emergency.

☐ Keep abreast of current conditions in the financial markets as the economy struggles through the recession so that you can manage your current portfolio effectively and make appropriate additional investments.

Tax Planning

☐ Review the 1990 tax law so that you'll know how it will affect you in 1991. Higher-income taxpayers will face higher tax bills. (See Appendix.)

☐ Familiarize yourself with tax-saving techniques so that you can increase your income by minimizing your income taxes.

Retirement Planning

☐ Continue contributing to your retirement plans (IRAs, 401(k) plans), and prepare projections to assure that you will be able to retire comfortably.

Other Matters

☐ If you have children in or about to enter college, review your plans for meeting college costs, and if necessary, revise them in light of your current financial situation. (See Chapter 23.)

☐ If you have elderly parents, encourage them to consult with you if they experience any financial problems as a result of the recession. (See Chapter Twenty-five.)

If you devote some time to reviewing the above matters, you will be in a much better position to anticipate recession-related problems and deal with them effectively, if and when they occur.

P A R T

II

COPING WITH
TOUGH ECONOMIC
TIMES

WHERE TO BEGIN—A DOZEN WINNING STRATEGIES TO PREPARE FOR TOUGH TIMES AHEAD

People in my community are really beginning to feel the effects of the economic decline. There was a layoff down at the plant. Sometimes I feel like we're just biding our time before something happens to us. I wish there was something we could do to prepare, but I haven't the faintest idea where to begin.

There are a lot of things you can and should do to protect you and your family from many of the financial problems that could arise during the recession. Some problems are probably beyond your control, like the loss of your job, reduced income, and investment setbacks. Others, however, can be avoided by realistic planning, and perhaps, some sacrifice. The dozen strategies that follow will help you take control of your financial future, so you can avoid the avoidable and survive the unavoidable. The following chapters discuss these strategies in more detail.

1. **Build up your savings.** One of the most important things you can do to protect yourself from the financial

adversity that will strike so many people during this recession is to build a cushion of savings to fall back on. In late 1990, the ranks of the unemployed were swelling by over 15,000 *per week*. Millions of additional workers may have their salaries frozen or even cut. Nothing can beat money in the bank (or in an accessible investment account) to help you shoulder these burdens, should they arise.

Another benefit of setting aside emergency funds is that you'll worry a lot less about what's going to happen to you and your family. If you have been saving regularly over the past few years, that's great. If you're particularly concerned about your financial well-being in 1991, you may want to increase your savings rate a bit. If you haven't been saving up to this point, it isn't too late to start. In fact, it is crucial that you begin to set aside some money—even a few dollars a week is better than nothing. For additional information about building up your savings, see Chapter Four.

2. **Get your debts under control.** Millions of people are choking on consumer debt. They're sitting on a house of cards—the slightest disruption in their personal financial situation, and they may be headed for big trouble. Whatever your debt situation, take the necessary steps to get your debts under control. First, don't add to your indebtedness. If necessary, take the scissors to your credit cards. Second, keep up to date on all of your obligations, and third, work to reduce your debts if they are excessive, even if it means putting your spending on a crash diet.

People with excessive debt have an awful lot to lose if they are victimized by the recession. People whose debts are under control may suffer a minor setback or two, but will emerge relatively unscathed and well prepared to take advantage of better economic times. Chapter Nine provides guidance on getting your debts under control.

3. **Maintain your good credit.** Whether you have a lot of debt, a little debt, or no debt, you need to maintain a good credit rating so that you can access credit if you need it during the coming tough times. Dipping into savings is preferable to incurring debt if your income drops, or if you have to meet unexpected expenses, but your circumstances may dictate that you temporarily have to borrow to make ends meet. Don't let poor credit make your life even more difficult. For more information on maintaining good credit, see Chapter Eight.

4. **Prepare budgets regularly.** You can bet most businesses are scrutinizing their budgets much more frequently and carefully during the current recession. You should be doing the same with your household budget. Revise it to reflect any actual or expected changes in your income or expenses. If you think something particularly troublesome might happen, such as temporary unemployment, prepare a budget that reflects that condition, so you can figure out what you'll need to do to make ends meet. Don't underestimate the importance of household budgeting. It is always useful, but it's essential during uncertain economic times. For more information on preparing budgets, see Chapter Five.

5. **Control your spending.** If there is one key to financial security, it is learning to live *beneath* your means. Until you get into the habit of spending less than you earn, you will never be able to accumulate a financial cushion to help weather economic uncertainty, much less be able to retire in comfort. Many people say it's impossible for them to save; that they only spend their money on absolute necessities and there is never anything left. Of course, you know as well as I do that they really haven't looked very hard at how and where they spend their money. There are ways to cut back spending, and they usually don't

cause a lot of pain. But it is far better to suffer a little pain now than it is to suffer a lot of pain later, if you're confronted with a financial emergency. If you still think it's impossible to cut down on your spending, Chapter Six lists 101 ways to reduce your expenses.

6. **Maintain your insurance coverage.** Unfortunately, many people reduce or eliminate essential insurance coverage when confronted with a personal money crisis. It seems to be a relatively painless thing to do. For example, they may drop their renter's or disability insurance policy, or they may decide to go without health insurance if they are laid off, rather than pay high premiums to maintain the coverage.

The problem with leaving even a single gap in your insurance coverage is that it exposes you to a possible uninsured loss, which could end up jeopardizing not only the assets that you currently own but also some of your future earnings. Chapter Ten discusses ways to assure that you have adequate insurance.

7. **Make your own investment decisions.** Coping with uncertain investment markets during a recession is a major concern. As a result, many investors tend to rely too much on the opinions and advice of others— more so than they would under more stable economic conditions. Investors who were managing perfectly well during normal markets end up in disarray during more turbulent markets.

While the opinions and advice of others may be helpful, you should be making your own investment decisions. That way, you'll understand what you're investing in and keep current on market conditions, both of which are essential if you're going to invest successfully in 1991. Chapter Sixteen recommends stocks and mutual funds for the recession.

8. **Maintain a balanced portfolio.** There is nothing like a bear market to cause investors to become preoccupied with short-term market performance. Of

course, it's no fun watching your portfolio decline in value, but down stock markets are inevitable and unpredictable. It is essential to avoid investing in extremes during a recession—liking stocks one week, loving bonds the next week, hating them both the next month. For more information on how to balance your investments, see Chapter Eleven.

9. **Select quality investments.** Don't make investments that don't make sense. Many people like to gamble with their investment money by selecting speculative stocks or investing in high-yield (junk) bonds. Certainly, some people can afford to speculate a little, but all too often they end up wasting their money on securities that are too risky. This recession already has devastated the prices of speculative investments. If the recession deepens, the devastation will continue. You should invest in only the highest-quality securities—those that can thrive in the worst economic circumstances. Weed lower-quality investments out of your portfolio now, and add only top-quality investments—blue-chip stocks or high-rated bonds. Chapters Thirteen, Fourteen, and Fifteen guide you in selecting high-quality stocks, interest-earning investments, and real estate, respectively.

10. **Anticipate any contingencies.** Don't deceive yourself during this recession. You need to review your current situation periodically, so you can anticipate any problems before they occur. These problems could include the loss of your job, salary freezes or reductions, credit problems, difficulty meeting your budget, or problems managing your investments. Uncertain times call for careful evaluation and planning: the sooner you anticipate the problem, the more time you have to address it. Part IV of this book contains several chapters that can assist you in anticipating and addressing problems that frequently occur during a recession.

11. **Get help if adversity strikes.** Millions of people are going to be adversely affected by this recession. Many will be reluctant to get the help that is available to assist them through trying times. Family financial problems often require tough choices, of course. But making tough choices is certainly preferable to letting your situation deteriorate even further. Several chapters of this book provide sources of assistance for financial problems you may encounter in the areas of insurance (Chapter 10), job loss (Chapter 17), credit problems (Chapter 21), mortgage problems (Chapter 24), problems meeting tuition costs (Chapter 23), problems of small business owners (Chapter 26), and bankruptcy (Chapter 28). Finally, remember the support that family members can provide during trying times (see Chapter 27).

12. **Be a survivor.** You *can* survive whatever adversity this recession throws your way. You probably know some people who have gone through tough times, who are doing just fine now. Many people have survived the sudden loss of their jobs, and many more will in 1991. They don't stay unemployed forever, and they usually end up with better jobs. Many people have lost their homes through foreclosure, and many more will in 1991. Most of them will be homeowners once again, and in a nicer home. Many people have suffered major financial losses during volatile stock and bond markets. They come back, too, with greater investment savvy and a larger portfolio. No matter how bad things get, you will be a survivor.

4

SAVING MORE NOW TO PROTECT YOU LATER

I have so many expenses these days, and it just seems that the cost of living goes up faster than my paycheck. I'm not even a big spender, but it's still impossible for me to save anything.

There is no better way to cope with the many potentially adverse effects of the recession than to have some money stashed away. Yet most of us have a great deal of difficulty saving, and as a result, we are unprepared for a financial crunch. Saving is not easy, but it is not impossible—and it is critical. Unless you plan to work for the rest of your life, worrying each day that the slightest glitch in your personal finances could be devastating, you need to save. Many people go through life thinking that Social Security and their company pension plan will stand them in good stead during their retirement years. This isn't so. Companies are cutting back on their pension plans, and your Social Security check will only get you through about one week of each month.

The nice thing about saving regularly is that it kills two birds with one stone. Not only does it prepare you for a comfortable retirement, but it also protects you against the financial troubles that we all experience during our working years. The current recession is going to teach many families a stern lesson. Those who have been savers will understand the importance of having resources available in the event of emergency. On the other hand, for nonsavers, the lesson could be very painful.

What are your savings habits? You probably fall into one of three categories.

- **Regular Savers.** Regular savers set aside money each week or month and enjoy the miracle of compounding earnings. Saving even modest amounts on a regular basis accumulates a lot of money over the years.
- **Erratic Savers.** This group always has good intentions, but generally has not yet developed a strategy for consistently putting money aside for the future.
- **Nonsavers.** Most nonsavers have good intentions as well. They know they need to save, but they simply can't get themselves into a position where this is possible. In the meantime, they live in constant fear that a financial calamity will befall them—loss of a job, big medical bills, or disability. A recession simply makes them even more anxious.

You Can Be a Better Saver

If you, like most people, find that you fall into the erratic saver or nonsaver category, you can learn to be a better saver. Certainly, it takes self-discipline, but saving regularly is essential, particularly since adversity could strike anyone during this economic slowdown. Don't think that it's too late to begin preparing for the 1991 recession. It's never too late to save, and if you are lucky enough to escape the effects of this economic downturn without being affected by it, you will be prepared for future financial adversities.

The first thing to do is to stop believing that you can't save any money, or that you can't save on a regular basis. This is not the case. Undoubtedly, there are people whose financial circumstances are almost identical to yours, who manage to save regularly. People who think it is impossible are avoiding the problem. Savers share one common characteristic: they have learned to live *beneath* their means. In other words, they spend less than they earn. It is that simple. You can't tell me that you absolutely, positively have to spend every cent you earn. If you want to become a better saver, or for that matter, a saver, you need to take two steps.

1. First, you have to find out where your money is going. By analyzing your spending habits carefully, you will undoubtedly find expenses that you can reduce or eliminate. Pay particular attention to how you spend your pocket money. Chances are that much of it is used on frivolous items. See Chapter Five for tips on how to summarize your past expenses.

2. Once you have identified areas where you can save money, the next step is to plan to save a fixed amount of money on a regular basis. The most painless way to do this is to "pay yourself first." In other words, have the money that you want to save automatically taken out of your paycheck or your checking account and placed in a savings or investment account. Since you never see the money, it is removed from temptation's reach. There are numerous ways that this can be accomplished through your employer, bank, mutual fund company, or stockbroker.

Even if you save only a few dollars a week, you will be surprised and comforted by how much you can accumulate over time. Putting $20 per week into a savings account earning 7 percent will accumulate

$1,100 in one year; a savings rate of $50 per week will amount to $2,700 in savings after just one year, and almost $40,000 in ten years!

How Much Should You Save?

Most Americans are abysmal savers, compared with citizens of other countries. Our national savings rate is a fraction of the savings rates of Japan and the Scandinavian countries. This doesn't mean that *you* have to be a poor saver. Virtually everyone can and should save at least 10 percent of his/her *gross* income. Once you get to that level, you should strive for a 15 percent to 20 percent savings level. Frankly, many people are going to have to save at a rate of 15 percent or higher if they are going to prepare a cushion against future financial emergencies and still realize their dream of retiring comfortably.

One question I am often asked is whether employees should contribute their own money to a company-sponsored retirement savings plan (a 401(k) plan, or in nonprofit organizations, a 403(b) plan). The answer is an emphatic "yes." These plans do count as savings, and it is essential that you maximize your contributions to these tax-advantaged retirement plans. On the other hand, you also need to set aside additional savings for personal use, particularly for short-term emergencies, which many people will experience during this recession. It may be very difficult, if not impossible, to gain access to your retirement plan contributions to handle personal needs.

So the time to start improving your savings program is now. Don't put it off. Even if you start with a very modest amount, you will begin to feel better about your financial future, and you will find that saving money isn't so painful after all. Sure, economic times are tough, but unless your current circumstances are particularly adverse (you've been laid off, for example), there is no reason to end or curtail your savings program. Use the following target savings work sheet to help you plan your savings program. You may find that saving 10 percent of your salary or gross income is simply not achievable at the present time. In the meantime, get into the habit of saving just a few dollars a week. Chapter Six contains 101 ways to reduce your expenses. If you follow some of them, you *will* be able to save money.

TARGET SAVINGS WORK SHEET

My weekly gross income is $_____

My weekly savings targets are:

Good (10% of gross weekly income)	$_____
Better (15% of gross weekly income)	$_____
Best (20% of gross weekly income)	$_____

IN ORDER TO SAVE MORE, YOU MUST

- [ ] Realize that you can;
- [ ] Analyze your spending habits, looking for expenses you can reduce or eliminate;
- [ ] Learn to spend less than you earn, in other words, live beneath your means;
- [ ] Save a fixed amount on a regular basis, ideally by "paying yourself first";
- [ ] Maximize contributions to company pension plans.

5

BUDGETING FOR TOUGH ECONOMIC TIMES

My paycheck just seems to disappear. I try to spend less, but it seems that as soon as I get my head above water, some new bill rolls in. How can I possibly save anything when I have all these bills to pay?

It's always hard to save money; but as times get tougher, your expenses may grow faster than your income, or your income may drop. It gets harder and harder to make ends meet, let alone to put anything away for the future. Almost everyone's saving and spending habits can be improved, but before you can change anything, you must familiarize yourself with your current spending patterns, so you can find out where you are spending and where you could be spending less. Businesses can't plan their spending without a budget. The only way for you to keep track of your spending so that you can control it is to prepare a budget, much like a budget that a business would prepare.

How Budgets Work

A budget will show you where your money is spent, so you can identify areas where you can reduce or eliminate unnecessary spending. If you're having trouble paying off your debts, showing creditors that you have a spending plan, including a realistic and well-thought-out budget, often will convince them to accept lower payments for a while, especially if you've been laid off or are otherwise under temporary financial duress.

A budget can help you plan how to use your hard-earned income most effectively, and how to maneuver your finances to attain certain goals that were otherwise unreachable. Preparing and maintaining a family budget can also help your peace of mind, because you'll have a much better idea of where you stand now and what you can do to minimize the effects of bad times ahead. Believe me, knowing the amount of income that you can expect, and how you are going to spend it, will go a long way toward easing the stress and family squabbles that often result from unforeseen financial burdens. If your finances ever deteriorate, your budget shows you where you can change things, so you can take action instead of feeling that matters are beyond your control.

Setting Up a Budget

Although setting up a system may appear burdensome, saving more money and having fewer money problems is something most people enjoy. Besides, it really isn't that hard to set up a simple budget that projects your income and expenses and allows you to keep track of how well you stay within those projections.

1. **Gather your records.** Unless you have some idea what you're spending now, you won't be able to set a budget for the future. Round up receipts, checkbooks, and bills that record your past expenditures. Divide

these into general categories to estimate how much you spent altogether. To estimate cash purchases, calculate the amount you spend in cash during a one-week or one-month period, and project that rate of spending over the period of time you want to budget. The following list may remind you of some areas where you spend. The list divides expenses you incur on a monthly basis from those you probably incur less frequently. Monthly bills budget themselves to a certain extent. It is much harder to plan to meet large, infrequent expenses.

2. **Analyze your past spending.** After you have sorted out your expenses for the last six months by category, compare the totals with the total amount of income you received during the same period. You might also want to divide each category's total by your total income, to determine what percentage of your income you spent on each category. If you spent more than 25 percent of your income on car payments, credit card bills, or other installment payments, chances are you're carrying too much consumer debt. Chapter Nine gives you some tips on getting those debts under control.

3. **Forecast your income.** Next, forecast your monthly cash income, including salary and income from savings and investments. Estimate realistically and conservatively, by referring to your income over the past year. Many people's income will be frozen or cut at some point during this recession, and you must be prepared if it happens to you. Some income typically is received on a monthly or more frequent basis, some less frequently but still regularly, and some sporadically. The next table may help you summarize your expected income from all sources.

4. **Prepare your budget.** After you have figured out how you have spent your income, you will be ready to budget your future expenses. Set expense targets for

SUMMARY OF PAST EXPENSES

Monthly expenses
Food .... $_____
Housing .... _____
Loan payments .... _____
Credit card payments .... _____
Maintenance .... _____
Saving .... _____
Household utilities and telephone .... _____
Medical and dental .... _____
Alimony/child support .... _____
Automobile/transportation .... _____
Clothing .... _____
Personal care .... _____
Entertainment and gifts .... _____
Miscellaneous cash expenses .... _____
Other _____ _____

Total $_____

**Expenditures typically incurred on a
less-than-monthly basis**
Estimated income taxes .... $_____
Property taxes .... _____
School tuition .... _____
Automobile insurance .... _____
Homeowner's/renter's insurance .... _____
Life insurance .... _____
Other insurance .... _____
Pension fund/IRA contributions .... _____
Automobile repairs and maintenance .... _____
Home repairs and maintenance .... _____
Seasonal fuel/electricity .... _____
Furniture purchases .... _____
Home improvements .... _____
Term loan repayments .... _____
Club dues and memberships .... _____
Vacations .... _____
Charitable donations .... _____
Holiday gifts .... _____
Cash gifts .... _____
Other _____ _____

Total $_____

SOURCES OF INCOME

**Income received on a monthly or
more frequent basis**
Salary $_____
Rent from investment property   _____
Alimony/child support   _____
Pension   _____
Social Security benefits   _____
Unemployment compensation   _____
Other _____   _____

**Income typically received on a less
frequent than monthly basis**
Bonus/profit-sharing $_____
Interest   _____
Dividends   _____
Income from sideline businesses   _____
Trust distributions   _____
Other _____   _____

Occasional income
Gifts $_____
Capital gains   _____
Sales of assets   _____
Other _____   _____

all items. Above all, be reasonable. While it is admirable to want to reduce your spending drastically, if you prepare a budget that you can't stick to, it won't do you any good at all.

Don't forget to account for irregular expenses, such as property taxes or vacations, in your budget. The best way to meet large, irregular expenses is to figure out how much they will be, when they will come due, and then to save for them in advance, perhaps in a separate savings account. That way you won't suffer a financial shock when those awful bills come rolling in.

The following budget work sheet can be used to prepare your budget.

5. **Record your expenses.** At the end of your budget period, record your actual expenses next to your projected expenses in the work sheet, so you can compare your actual expenses with the targets you set. Ideally, you should do this frequently and revise your projections as necessary. Unfortunately, preparing a budget is easy; sticking to it can be hard. Making a budget doesn't give you more money, but sticking to it should.

6. **Account for contingencies.** You may need to adjust your budget from time to time to reflect any changes in your financial circumstances that the recession causes. Perhaps your income is not going to be as high as you originally expected; or some expenses, like gas and fuel oil, may increase more than you originally budgeted.

Making It Work

Anyone who has ever tried to lose weight knows that no matter what menu you draw up, you won't get any thinner until you diet. Putting your spending on a diet is just the same. No matter how much fat you cut out of your budget, you won't see any results unless you can keep your actual spending just as lean. A successful budget carefully balances economic responsibilities with the dynamics of family relationships. All family members involved must agree on the basic allotment of funds, or the budget will not work. Set reasonable spending limits, and leave a comfortable margin for unexpected expenses. It's also a good idea to budget a personal allowance that need not be accounted for, for each family member. This gives

---

BUDGET WORK SHEET

This budget covers the following time period: _____

	Estimated Future Amounts	Actual Amounts*
Income		
Gross salary	$_____	$_____
Investment income	_____	_____
Other income	_____	_____
Total income	$_____	$_____
Essential expenses		
Income taxes	$_____	$_____
Rent/mortgage	_____	_____
Home heating	_____	_____
Electricity	_____	_____
Natural gas	_____	_____
Water	_____	_____
Garbage collection	_____	_____
Telephone	_____	_____
Loan payments	_____	_____
Tuition payments	_____	_____
Property taxes	_____	_____
Auto insurance	_____	_____
Other insurance	_____	_____
Medical, dental	_____	_____
Savings	_____	_____
Other: _____	_____	_____
Total essential expenses	$_____	$_____
Expenses over which you have some control		
Food, alcohol, tobacco	$_____	$_____
Household maintenance	_____	_____
Furnishings, equipment	_____	_____
Clothing	_____	_____
Transportation	_____	_____
Personal care, grooming	_____	_____
Recreation	_____	_____
Contributions, donations	_____	_____
Gifts	_____	_____
Laundry, dry cleaning	_____	_____
Other: _____	_____	_____
Total discretionary expenses	$_____	$_____
Grand total of expenses	$_____	$_____
Amount that income exceeds or falls short of expenses	$_____	$_____

*Fill in this column at the end of the time period budgeted for so you can compare actual amounts of income and expenses against what you budgeted.

everyone some limited financial freedom to pursue individual tastes.

Consider the budget as a control mechanism—a tool to synchronize your actions with your plans. The positive, secure feelings created by the time and effort expended are well worth it—especially now, when financial peace of mind doesn't come easily.

Essentials, Luxuries, and Savings

What if you keep looking at the numbers, and no matter how you slice it you see you've been spending more than you're earning? Well, that was the common way of life in the extravagant eighties. When the economy seemed like it was going to keep expanding forever, many people, like many companies, overexpanded. They spent money on the assumption that it would keep coming in faster and faster. Now the hardtimes nineties have hit, and many people are having difficulty paying off the debts of their past excesses. The more income you have, the more you want to buy with it. No amount of income will be enough. If you want something badly enough, you will sacrifice other things for it. Unfortunately, the thing you want so badly is often frivolous or excessive. Your budget is the place to determine whether something is essential or a luxury. For example, cosmetics and clothing may be essentials, but designer-label cosmetics and clothing are luxuries. If you have trouble distinguishing between luxuries and necessities, review Chapter Six.

Your budget is the place to decide what is really important to you and how you are going to pay for it. If your income isn't sufficient to cover your projected expenses, you're going to have to make some hard choices. When deciding which expenses you can live without, remember that personal saving is an essential expense. Treat it as such, and budget for savings the same way you budget for other essential expenses, such as rent or mortgage payments.

TO BUDGET FOR ROUGH TIMES AHEAD:

- ☐ Summarize your past experiences and income.
- ☐ Project your income and expenses over the next year, taking the recession into consideration.
- ☐ Leave extra room for savings to cushion any ugly surprises from the recession.
- ☐ Recognize that you will have to spend less in some areas to meet your objectives. Identify areas where you can reduce spending.
- ☐ Stay within your target spending.

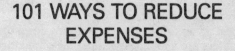

6

101 WAYS TO REDUCE EXPENSES

Our friends are so much better at shopping and controlling their expenses than we are. They always seem to have money left over, while we always seem to be running short toward the end of the month. Do they know something we don't?

Most people are beginning to feel pinched during the current recession, and it is likely that things will be worse in 1991. Many of us will have to cut back in order to build up a financial cushion to weather the storm that is ahead. Others will have to cut back on expenses just to make ends meet. This chapter lists 101 ways that you can reduce your expenses. Check off the ones that apply to you. I'll guarantee that if you review this list, you will find some not-too-painful ways to cut back. By the way, there is no law that says you have to raise living expenses when prosperity returns.

☐ **1. Cut down on gift giving.** Don't accuse me of being Ebenezer Scrooge. The plain fact is that most of us spend more on gifts during the holidays and throughout the year than we should. The price of a gift is not a measure of the depth of the love that we have for our loved ones. Instead of spending a bucket of money, be more imaginative. Also, you'll know that you've got control of your personal finances when you spend at the same rate between Thanksgiving and Christmas as you do between Christmas and Thanksgiving.

☐ 2. **Put on an extra sweater, and turn down the heat.** Sweaters are a lot cheaper than the oil, natural gas, or electricity that you use to heat your home.

☐ 3. **Buy energy-efficient light bulbs.** You won't go blind using energy-efficient light bulbs; they're just as bright. Besides, your eyes will take comfort next time you look at your electricity bill.

☐ 4. **Appeal your property tax assessment.** Surprisingly, a large percentage of people who appeal their property tax assessments end up with a lower bill. Don't forget, property values already have dropped in many areas of the country and will drop in many more as the recession continues.

☐ 5. **Buy no-load mutual funds.** I can't understand why people want to pay someone to recommend a mutual fund when, with very little effort, you could select an equivalent or better fund with no sales commission.

☐ 6. **Buy a water saver for your shower.** You probably can pick up a water saver free from a local utility. You won't even know the difference after you install it.

☐ 7. **Brown bag it at work.** This doesn't mean that you should bring alcohol in a plain bag to work, although the way the economy is going you may be tempted to. Instead, start bringing your lunch to work. Have you ever calculated how much you spend on lunch at work, over the course of a year? It's probably the equivalent of one month's rent or mortgage payment. Sure, the cafeteria manager or local deli is not going to appreciate my telling you this, but I'm more concerned that you survive this recession and achieve financial security. Bringing your lunch can be a major step in that direction.

☐ 8. **Leave the car at home, and use public transportation.** You can save a bundle by taking public transportation rather than driving to work. It is not a sign of poverty to use public transportation; it's a sign of good sense.

☐ 9. **Find a good dry cleaner.** It's amazing how many people will put up with cleaners that burn their shirts or break their buttons. Believe it or not, it is possible to have your shirts laundered properly. Why pay to have them ruined?

☐ 10. **Buy generic groceries.** You probably think that generic groceries are inherently inferior. Have you tried them? You can always go back to wasting your money on more expensive brands if your taste buds are offended.

☐ 11. **Quit playing the lottery.** Lotteries are nothing more than a tax on the naive. They are a complete waste of money, and the people who spend the most on them can least afford to do so. You might as well throw that money in the fireplace. At least then it will then provide you with some heat.

☐ 12. **Keep your cars longer.** There's no reason why you can't keep a car for seven to ten years or even longer. People who trade their cars in every three, four, or five years are simply throwing money away. Sure, a late model car feels good, and you probably think people are impressed by it. But is it worth the cost?

☐ 13. **Save restaurants for special occasions.** Americans are restaurant addicts. If you're inclined to pinch pennies, curb your restaurant habit.

☐ 14. **Rent movies instead of going out to the movies.**

Unless you feel compelled to see the latest movies, rent them and bring them home. Have you noticed that movie theater ticket prices keep rising and movie rental prices keep dropping? There's a message in there for you.

☐ 15. **Move out of the city.** If you are an urban dweller, consider the suburbs. Although you may have to weigh the lower housing costs against the costs of commuting, you could save quite a bit.

☐ 16. **Refinance your mortgage at a lower rate.** If mortgage interest rates drop one percent or more below the current rate on your mortgage, figure out how much money you could save by refinancing. It may be worth the cost.

☐ 17. **Check your newspaper for great deals on used furniture.** You can get some amazing bargains by buying used furniture through the newspaper. Hint: in responding to the ad, find out where the seller lives. If it's a fancy neighborhood, get over there fast to look at the furniture.

☐ 18. **Cut down on your dry cleaning.** Don't take your clothes to be dry cleaned just because they're wrinkled. Opt for "press only," or better yet, iron them yourself.

☐ 19. **Raise the deductibles on your insurance policies.** You can save hundreds of dollars by raising the deductibles on your automobile and homeowner's or renter's insurance policies. More on this in Chapter Ten.

☐ 20. **Go to resorts in the off season.** If you play your cards right, you can visit a resort just before the season rates begin or just after they end. You might enjoy a less-crowded resort when you visit in the off season, and you'll certainly enjoy the money you save.

☐ 21. **Use campgrounds rather than hotels for vacations.** You'll be healthier for it.

☐ 22. **Take care of your tires to save your car.** Rotate your tires regularly, and check the air in your tires every time you get gas. Even if you pay to have these simple tasks done, it'll help you avoid replacing expensive tires prematurely.

☐ 23. **Buy generic drugs.** Generic drugs can save you a lot of money. In many instances they are identical to those with brand names. Your physician or pharmacist will be glad to help you decide when to choose the generic. If you want to save even more money, you can buy generics through the mail.

☐ 24. **Find a good tailor.** Do you buy new clothes when you still have clothes whose lapels are too wide or whose hemlines are too long? Ask your tailor to take them in or take it up. It'll be like buying a new item for the cost of the alteration.

☐ 25. **Slow down.** Driving at the speed limit not only improves your gas mileage, but it also avoids the expense (and annoyance) of those nasty moving violations.

☐ 26. **Keep meticulous tax records.** Unless you want to pay more taxes than you have to, improve your tax record-keeping system. Keep a notebook handy to keep track of miscellaneous tax-deductible expenses.

☐ 27. **Eat at cheaper restaurants.** There are marvelous restaurants in your community that serve good food, have good service, and charge a lot less than you're used to paying for a night on the town.

☐ 28. **Sell your second (or third) car.** Do you really need so many cars? Do you remember the days when families got along perfectly well with one, or at most, two cars? I know people who have two drivers in the family who own three, four, or as many as five cars! What's going on?

☐ 29. **Turn down the air-conditioning.** You can save a lot of money in hotter climes by running the air conditioner a little less. In many areas, fans make more sense except on the hottest days.

☐ 30. **Find a good cobbler.** Fix your old shoes before buying new ones. Also ask about preventive steps you can take to keep your shoes from wearing down and wearing out.

☐ 31. **Take the train or bus instead of a plane.** Unless you are going a long distance or are pressed for time, consider alternatives to airplanes. It seems like the airlines are raising prices almost daily. They must be paying sixty dollars per gallon for jet fuel. Trains or buses may not add that much time to the trip; you'll save money; and you'll also be able to enjoy a seat that, unlike an airplane seat, is more than six inches wide.

☐ 32. **Decide what you're buying before you go shopping, and resist impulse purchases.** How many times have you gone off to the shopping center to buy a fifteen dollar item, and ended up lightening your pocketbook by two hundred dollars? You know you shouldn't do it, but you do. Try to resist impulse purchases; and remember, when you save money by buying something on sale, you really haven't saved money, you've spent it.

☐ 33. **Wash and wax your car yourself, instead of taking it to the car wash.** It really doesn't take that much time and effort to wash and wax your car periodically. The exercise is good for you, too, and since you'll be more fit, you'll live longer and be able to enjoy the money you saved by not enriching the local car wash.

☐ 34. **Use discount brokers.** If you want to make good investment decisions, make them yourself, and when you do so, use discount brokerage firms. They'll save you a lot of money on commissions, and they won't call you at dinnertime to recommend that you buy "Nikkei put warrants," or some other get-poor-quickly investment.

☐ 35. **Buy your next pet from an animal shelter (around $25) instead of a pet store (around $300) or a breeder.** It'll love you just as much, and probably cost you less to maintain than some rare purebred that probably has bad eyes and bad hips.

☐ 36. **Tear up your credit cards.** This is one of the all-time great ways to save money. I suggest you do it with great pomp and circumstance. Afterward, treat yourself to something, but remember, you'll have to pay cash.

☐ 37. **Buy in bulk quantities, but only if you'll use it all.** True, it's more expensive up front to buy in bulk, but it is a great way to save on staples and dry goods.

☐ 38. **Put away your checkbook.** The greater the distance you can place between yourself and your checkbook (not to mention your credit cards), the less temptation there will be to write a check for something you don't need.

☐ 39. **Never go grocery shopping on an empty stomach.** This is an inviolable law. You'll buy fewer groceries, and you won't risk serious physical injury from trying to carry five hundred pounds of groceries into your kitchen in a weakened condition.

☐ 40. **Get take-out instead of eating in the restaurant.** Sure, it doesn't have the ambience, but you'll save on tipping, and you can provide your own drinks. If the take-out joint is close by, walk over and pick it up instead of paying for delivery.

☐ 41. **Buy a good used car rather than an expensive new car.** The quickest way to lose $2,000 is to drive a new car off the dealer's lot. So many people are obsessed with frequently trading in their cars, there are many excellent used cars that go begging. If you get into the habit of buying used cars, you'll save literally tens of thousands of dollars over your lifetime.

☐ 42. **Buy term rather than cash-value life insurance.** I don't want to get into the raging controversy over which is better, term or cash-value insurance, but I can say that term insurance is cheaper in the short run than cash-value, despite what the person who desperately wants to sell you a cash-value policy will say. If you're concerned about providing the most insurance coverage for the lowest cost now, buy term.

☐ 43. **Stay away from designer labels on everything from clothes to cosmetics.** No wonder clothing designers and cosmetics mavens live in baronial splendor. Have you seen how much they charge for their products? Believe me, eschewing these overpriced products will not consign you to a life of ill-clad ugliness.

☐ 44. **Take advantage of bargains and sales when you need an item.** The problem, of course, is that when we see something on sale, we automatically assume we need it. But if you genuinely need something, by all means try to purchase it at the lowest price.

☐ 45. **Contribute to an IRA and other retirement-oriented plans.** Obviously, this doesn't save you money up front, but since the income from these investments is not taxed until you retire, it will save you taxes year-in and year-out. You need to contribute to these plans anyway, if you want to retire comfortably.

☐ 46. **Don't be taken in by promotions.** For example, don't subscribe to a magazine because they'll give you a free clock radio or a videotape of athletes doing stupid things. If you want a clock radio, buy a clock radio, not a magazine.

☐ 47. **If it sounds too good to be real, it is.** Don't buy *anything* that guarantees to make you money without having to work for it, to lose weight without dieting, or to grow hair where no hair grows.

☐ 48. **Take the scissors to your ATM card.** This may be an extreme action, but if you find that you are frittering away a lot of your pocket cash and you're going to your ATM machine constantly to withdraw money—and many banks charge a fee each time you make a withdrawal—then saying goodbye to the card will mean that you can only get cash during banking hours.

☐ 49. **Stock up during seasonal sales.** Many seasonal sales are genuine sales. If you are good at planning ahead, you can save by taking advantage of a retailer's excess inventory.

☐ 50. **Don't pay extra for extra ingredients.** Paying for soap with moisturizer, for example, or cereal with raisins is almost always considerably more expensive than buying soap and moisturizer or cereal and raisins separately. There are never enough raisins in the cereal with raisins anyway.

☐ 51. **Buy at discount clothing centers.** You'd be surprised at how many of your better-dressed acquaintances aren't paying full price for their perfectly good clothes.

☐ 52. **Turn off the lights when you leave the room.** Unless you own stock in the local electric utility, you're not doing your finances any good by leaving lights burning all over your home.

☐ 53. **Join a carpool.** Isn't it a bit ridiculous to waste all that money driving to work alone 250 times per year?

☐ 54. **Quit smoking.** Smoking is dangerous to your financial health. The habit can easily cost over $1,000 per year, not to mention what it does to your health and life insurance premiums, cleaning bills, and dental bills.

☐ 55. **Clip and use coupons.** You'll be amazed how those nickels and dimes add up. Some coupon experts save hundreds of dollars per year on groceries.

☐ 56. **Take vacations closer to home.** There are probably great places to vacation near your hometown. Many people live close to vacation areas that other people travel hundreds or thousands of miles to visit.

☐ 57. **Drop the collision coverage from your automobile insurance policy on an old car.** Some people who have old cars pay almost as much for their collision coverage as the car is worth.

☐ 58. **Avoid shopping at convenience stores.** Unless you prefer to pay outrageous prices for staples, do your grocery shopping at the grocery store. You'll save money on food, and you'll avoid the tempting lottery machines.

☐ 59. **Read the label.** Always follow storage and care instructions on clothing and food. Spoilage and discards are money down the drain.

☐ 60. **Be wary of anything "free."** Somehow, everything that's free ends up costing you money.

☐ 61. **Don't carry excess cash.** Rather than carry a lot of cash around, roll up a $50 or $100 traveler's check and hide it in the deepest recesses of your wallet, only to be used in an emergency. All too often, the extra cash people carry for "emergencies" ends up being spent on frivolities. You'll be less tempted to dig out and cash your traveler's check.

☐ 62. **Pump your own gas.** Gas is too expensive to begin with, so why pay extra to have someone pump the liquid gold into your chariot?

☐ 63. **Shop at food warehouses instead of supermarkets.** Some grocery stores are cheaper than others, and food warehouses are often the cheapest of all.

64. **Pay off your entire credit card bill every month.** Consumer credit incurs just about the steepest interest rates of any debt. Pay your bills every month and spare yourself the finance charges, which are no longer tax deductible.

65. **Subscribe to fewer cable stations, or cancel your service altogether.** Television is a necessity, and it can be a welcome diversion, but do you need 350 channels?

66. **Finance cars over three years or less.** Some people never manage to get out from under a car loan. If you can't afford to finance a car over two or three years, you can't afford that car.

67. **Prepare your own tax returns.** The best way to learn how to save taxes is to prepare your own tax returns. The IRS provides many free pamphlets and there are many books on the market that can help you out.

68. **Moderate your drinking.** That may be a little extreme, but you can still cut your liquor bills considerably by sticking to wine and beer and keeping it local. Many fine products are made in America. You don't need to pay a fortune on German beer and French wine.

69. **Make your airline reservations well in advance.** The cheapest airline fares go fast, so plan ahead and make your reservations as soon as your plans are firm.

70. **Don't get sick.** Preventive medicine is the cheapest medicine. Learn how to stay healthy, so you can spend all of the money you save.

71. **Put your kids on a budget.** Make your children account for where they spend their allowance. If they become wise spenders, you will save money in the long run because they won't need to ask you for so much.

72. **Learn to perform routine car maintenance your-**

self. Have you noticed the labor charges for car maintenance and repairs lately? While not quite up there with neurosurgeons' fees, they're getting there. You can perform more routine maintenance tasks on your car than you think.

☐ 73. **Stay over a Saturday night on airline trips.** Airfares are generally much cheaper if you stay over a Saturday night. The extra night in a hotel is usually a fraction of the airfare savings.

☐ 74. **Cut the kids' hair yourself.** Nobody can get young children to sit still long enough to give them good haircuts, so why not do it yourself?

☐ 75. **Always try to do it yourself before paying someone else to do it.** Unless the task is dangerous, this advice holds true for home repairs and minor renovations, cleaning, plumbing, car maintenance, tax preparation, and laundry.

☐ 76. **Wear glasses instead of contacts.** Even fairly expensive glasses with scratch-proof, ultraviolet-resisting lenses will cost you less over the long run than the hundreds of little vials of solutions you'll need to clean your contact lenses. Besides, you probably won't tear or lose your glasses.

☐ 77. **Use sponges more and paper towels less.** How can they make paper towel rolls that last less than a day so thick? Resist the Pavlovian response to go to the paper towel roll. Instead, reach for the sponge.

☐ 78. **Write letters to long-distance friends instead of calling them.** What ever happened to our letter-writing habits, anyway? Your friends will be impressed by your resourcefulness and touched by your thoughtfulness. The only one who might take offense is Ma Bell.

☐ 79. **Never run the dishwasher unless it's full.** It costs the same either way.

☐ 80. **Buy mass transit discount passes and toll vouchers to reduce commuting costs. The savings might seem trivial to you, but they sure do add up.

☐ 81. **Return your bottles and cans so that you can get your deposit back.** Sure it's inconvenient, but you're making a trip to the grocery store anyway, and the nickels add up over time. Do you realize that if you returned twenty million cans at a nickel apiece, you'd be a millionaire?

☐ 82. **Join consumer "buying clubs."** As long as you truly need the item, search for the least expensive way to purchase it. Consumer buying clubs may be the ticket.

☐ 83. **Make your long-distance calls at night and on weekends.** Some people think that since long-distance rates drop all the time they can afford the luxury of calling whenever the mood strikes them. The cheapest times to call are typically between 11:00 p.m. and 8:00 a.m. each night, all day Saturday, and all day Sunday, except from 5:00 p.m. to 11:00 p.m. You can save a lot, particularly if you talk a lot.

☐ 84. **Turn off the television when you're not in the room.** If you want to have noise on in the house to keep you company or fend off burglars, keep the radio on, not the television.

☐ 85. **Cancel your subscriptions to newspapers or magazines you don't read.** If you don't read it, you don't need it.

☐ 86. **Help your children make cards and gifts for their friends instead of buying them.** You can become impoverished buying greeting cards these days. The homemade variety are preferable, anyway, particularly for kids.

☐ 87. **Use the phone book before calling directory assistance.** Directory assistance can cost big money! Check your phone bill to see how much you use directory assistance. I've never been able to figure out why some people are too lazy to look it up in the phone book.

☐ 88. **Seek alternatives to health clubs.** Unless you go to a health club to socialize, it can be a very expensive way to exercise. Cut your exercise costs by purchasing your own equipment—used equipment is a steal—using a public pool or gym, going for a run in the park, or joining the local YMCA or JCC at a nominal cost.

☐ 89. **Don't get credit life insurance.** Credit life insurance, in other words insurance you buy from a lender to pay off a loan or mortgage in case you die, is almost always a rip-off. If you do need the insurance, it is cheaper to buy it yourself.

☐ 90. **Don't let your children watch Saturday morning cartoons on network TV.** Sure, it's nice that the children are occupied on Saturday mornings so you can sleep in, but do you realize how many commercials they are being bombarded with? They will hit you up with requests for toys that were advertised on these programs, the aggregate value of which would approach the GNP of some small countries.

☐ 91. **Increase the waiting period on your disability insurance.** If you have purchased your own disability income insurance policy, ask your agent to quote you rates on a longer waiting period, perhaps six months or one year. The waiting period is the time between the onset of your disability and the time you begin collecting the benefits. The longer the waiting period, the lower the premiums.

☐ 92. **Buy it to last.** Many people seem to have forgotten that *non*disposable razors and *cloth* napkins even exist. These items will cost you more than their short-lived counterparts in the short-term, but once you're equipped, they'll save you money for some time.

☐ 93. **Take advantage of senior citizen discounts.** If you are age sixty-five or older, you can take advantage of numerous discounts available to senior citizens. You may have to do a little digging to find them. Be sure to ask your friends what senior citizen discounts they are aware of.

☐ 94. **Take advantage of discounts on auto and homeowner's insurance.** You may qualify for any number of discounts that are available on automobile and homeowner's insurance policies. Check with your agent to find out what discounts are available and which ones you qualify for.

☐ 95. **Make your children's Halloween costumes instead of buying them.** Let your child use some imagination; you'll save some money.

☐ 96. **Don't send packages via first-class mail.** Unless it is urgent, use parcel post rather than first class or priority mail to send packages.

☐ 97. **Buy family members gifts that they need.** Sure, it may not be so romantic, but if your husband needs a chain saw, why not give it to him for his birthday? This tough economy is hardly the time to bedeck your honey with expensive jewelry anyway.

☐ 98. **Try to lose weight on your own.** Consult with a doctor, buy a couple of diet books, and really try to lose weight on your own before going to an expensive weight-loss clinic. The one thing that's certain about a weight-loss clinic is that they'll certainly put your wallet on a diet.

☐ 99. **Rent an RV rather than buying one.** Unless you are retired and are going to travel throughout the year, you are probably better off renting a recreational vehicle for your vacations and periodic sojourns rather than buying one. They're an eyesore in your driveway anyway.

☐ 100. **Same goes for boats.**

☐ 101. **Ask to be cremated.** While you won't enjoy any benefits from this expense-saving tactic, your heirs will.

7

FIFTEEN WAYS TO INCREASE YOUR INCOME

I sure could use a little extra money. I guess everyone could, but these oil prices are going to be the death of me yet. I have a long commute, and if that weren't bad enough, my heating oil bill is astronomical this year. If I could make a little more money, I could pay those bills and start to set a little bit aside so that I wouldn't have to worry the next time I get an unexpected jolt.

Sometimes, a little extra money can spell the difference between desperation and financial peace of mind. Many industrious people have found ways to increase their income in order to meet living expenses or increase their savings. Fifteen ways to increase your income are listed below. Some of the strategies will provide small amounts of money, which may be all you need to meet a particularly pressing financial obligation or balance your budget. Others can add considerable cash to your coffers.

☐ 1. **Moonlight.** Moonlighting is perhaps the best way for many people to augment their income. You may be able to take a part-time job in the evening or on weekends. You may have a skill, such as painting or word processing, that you can turn into a lucrative part-time business. If you look around, you will find ample moonlighting opportunities, and as long as they don't jeopardize your full-time work, you can supplement your job income nicely. Incidentally, if you do moonlight, you may be able to take advantage of certain tax breaks for self-employed people, including the opportunity to set up your own retirement plan.

☐ 2. **Shift investments into higher-yielding securities.** If your investments are concentrated in stocks, or if you have cash that's sitting in your checking account, you can increase your current income by moving money into higher-yielding interest-earning securities, like money market funds and CDs. But be careful of investments that promise an unusually high yield, since high yield means high risk.

☐ 3. **Take in a boarder or a roommate.** You could add hundreds of dollars to your monthly income by taking in a roommate. Admittedly, this isn't everyone's cup of tea, but tough financial times may call for a temporary change of lifestyle. If you have adult children living with you who are employed, they should be paying you room and board. If my three-year-old daughter had any money, you can bet I would charge her room and board.

☐ 4. **Have a yard sale.** A yard sale is a great way to get rid of items you no longer need, and to raise some money. Even the best neighborhoods have yard sales. In addition, if you no longer need some major possessions, such as furniture, place an ad in the local paper.

☐ 5. **Buy items at yard sales and resell them to dealers or at flea markets.** Some people make big money buying "junk" at yard sales and selling them as "antiques" to dealers or at flea markets. These people have an eye for value and a knack for identifying collectibles in someone's front yard. You can make thousands of dollars a year by doing this. I know a woman who bought an original Rembrandt etching for $10 at a yard sale. It was worth $25,000!

☐ 6. **Buy municipal bonds.** You can probably increase your interest income by selling taxable bonds and buying municipal bonds. After factoring in federal and state taxes, lower-yielding municipal bonds provide you with more income than taxable securities like CDs and government bonds.

☐ 7. **Take out a second mortgage, or refinance your first mortgage for a higher amount.** This strategy should not be taken lightly since it could jeopardize your home. Unless your situation is desperate, it is unwise to use home equity financing to meet current living expenses or to make unnecessary purchases. This is doubly true in the current uncertain economic environment.

☐ 8. **File your tax return early if you are due a refund.** Although you may be in the habit of filing your tax return at the last minute, the sooner you file, the sooner you will get any refund you are due. So, unless you feel it is your patriotic duty to let the government have your money for a few extra months, file your tax return early.

☐ 9. **Adjust your withholding.** Are you sure you aren't having too much money withheld from your paycheck for taxes? If you got a refund last year, if you are going to have higher deductible expenses this year, or if your income may drop this year, you may be able to increase the number of your withholding exemptions in order to decrease the taxes withheld. It's not that difficult to figure out, and it's worth it if you can increase your take-home pay during these tough times.

☐ 10. **Shop around for the best yields on interest-earning investments.** Next time your CD comes due, don't simply roll it over without comparing the new interest rate with rates offered by other banks and financial institutions. You may be surprised to find that by transferring your money to another institution you can increase your interest income. Your CD world is no longer limited to your hometown. Brokerage firms, including the discounters, now have "CD shopping services" that scour the nation to find the highest CD rates. As long as your CD is in a federally insured institution, it doesn't matter whether it's on deposit in a bank down the street or two thousand miles away.

☐ 11. **Move to a state with lower taxes.** Many people are beginning to realize that some states have much higher tax burdens than others. If you are young, or if you otherwise have some flexibility as to where you live, consider moving to a state where there is both opportunity and lower taxes.

☐ 12. **Collect income from your favorite charity.** No, I'm not suggesting that you ask for charity, but if you are charitably inclined, you can donate cash or securities to your favorite charity in return for a lifetime income. What's more, these so-called charitable remainder trusts, pooled income funds, and charitable gift annuities will provide you with a partial tax deduction for your donation. It's like having your cake and eating it too. They sound complicated, but if you contact your favorite charity, they'll be happy to tell you all you need to know about these programs.

☐ 13. **Work part-time.** Many people who are not currently in the work force, like homemakers, retired people, students, and the temporarily unemployed

are finding that there's an abundance of part-time
jobs available to augment family income. Many
companies are effectively utilizing part-time employees, and in order to attract them, offer flexible
working arrangements and working hours.

☐ 14. **Reduce your contributions to your company
401(k) plan or other savings/thrift plans.** This action
should only be considered a temporary solution to
increase your take-home pay to meet a short-term
financial problem. Hopefully, you will be able to
restore these important retirement plan contributions as soon as your financial situation stabilizes.

☐ 15. **Sell investments.** You can increase your income
by selling some investments, but this should be
viewed as only a temporary expedient, since you
should be adding to your investments, not reducing
them. But one of the comforting aspects of having
money in the bank is that you can gain access to it
in the event of a personal financial emergency.
Selling investments can extend to cashing in IRAs
or other retirement plans, but only as a last resort.
Not only will you incur stiff penalties, but you'll
also jeopardize your retirement security.

8

GETTING AND MAINTAINING GOOD CREDIT

I've always tried to pay all my debts on time, but it's getting harder and harder. I don't think I've borrowed excessively. Won't my past record see me through a few little problems?

In a recession, a good credit rating can be the key to seeing you through a financial emergency. In the current economic slump, keeping yourself in the black is going to get harder. If your borrowing and spending are in reasonably good shape, that's great. Unfortunately, a good credit rating is a lot easier to lose than it is to achieve, and establishing and maintaining a good credit record is hard even in the most prosperous economic environment.

During these trying times, it is crucial that you maintain your good credit and the capacity to increase your borrowing, if necessary, in case of an emergency. However, that doesn't mean it's all right to keep running up debts, or borrow for nonessential purchases. Interest on debt used to save you quite a bit on your taxes. But consumer indebtedness, which includes just about all kinds of debt except home mortgages and investment loans, is no longer tax deductible beginning in 1991. Even debt that still is tax deductible doesn't save much in taxes anymore, since tax rates are much lower than they used to be. Any way you look at it, debt is less attractive than it used to be, but judging by the ever-increasing level of credit card indebtedness, that hasn't deterred many people from borrowing. In fact, a recent study indicated that American consumer debt as a percentage of disposable income is at its highest level since World War II. The conclusion: Americans are using debt to support their comfortable lifestyles.

Good Debt and Bad Debt

Debt can be very beneficial, or it can be detrimental. Just as there's a difference between essential spending and frivolous spending, there are good reasons to borrow and bad reasons to borrow. If you list your current loans and what they were used to purchase, you will be able to make that distinction easily. If you've always been able to pay off your debts, you may begin to feel that borrowing is the easiest way to purchase something. But as it gets harder to pay your debts, it's time to decide when you just shouldn't borrow. You probably didn't really need many of the items you purchased with plastic, anyway. With the way the economy is heading, this is a good time to rein in your spending.

The best way to manage personal debt is to borrow only for appropriate reasons and to pay off those loans within a reasonable period of time. Good debt finances something worthwhile, which will benefit you well into the future. Bad debt usually finances something that you use up almost immediately or that you never receive any real benefit from—borrowing to consolidate loans, for example. Thus, a home mortgage is good debt, and credit card indebtedness is almost always bad debt. Borrowing to invest can be good or bad, depending on how the investment fares, but right now it's probably not a great idea, because chances are your interest payments will exceed the return on your investment, at least near term.

Establishing Your Creditworthiness

If you're trying to establish your creditworthiness for the first time, you may be frustrated by rejections. Even people with good jobs and respectable backgrounds often are turned down if they haven't borrowed in the past. Current economic conditions combined with the pervasive woes of the banking industry make it even tougher for first-time borrowers to establish their credit. It seems ironic that you have to incur debt in order to prove you can handle debt. But it's worth pursuing; a sound credit rating can be a godsend in an emergency. Those rejections don't go on your credit record, by the way, so keep trying and good luck.

If your income is relatively low but steady, it may be more difficult for you to qualify for a loan, but it still is possible. Lenders are much more sympathetic to borrowers who show their fiscal responsibility and who are borrowing for worthwhile purposes, such as buying a home. Many lower-income people do qualify for a mortgage through hard work, saving, and if available, participation in various community programs that facilitate home ownership for moderate-income individuals and families.

How to Maintain Credit

All loans should be paid off as soon as possible—ideally, long before the asset you purchased with the loan stops benefitting you. Car loans are a special case, since they involve borrowing to buy a depreciating asset. Therefore, a car should be financed over no more than two to three years, although the average car loan length now approaches five years. If you borrow for much more than two years, you will start incurring repair bills while you're still making loan payments—hardly an appealing situation. If you can't afford to finance a car over three years or less, you can't really afford that car. Young people typically spend more to own and maintain a car than they do on housing. No wonder they can't seem to save up enough to make a downpayment on a home! If you find yourself constantly saddled with car loans, do some serious thinking about how much it is costing you to drive around in your steel and plastic master. I prefer old, unappealing cars. They're a lot cheaper in the long run, and I'd rather put my money to more productive use. Sure, people may laugh at my old clunker. Once, a neighbor even put the following "ticket" on my 12-year-old car: "Your car violates this neighborhood's standards of good taste." Was I bothered by that? Not for one second, because by not wasting my money on fancy, late-model cars, I was able to afford to live in that neighborhood.

Developing a personal relationship with your banker is a good way to preserve your credit, as times get tougher for both you and the bank. Individuals who discuss their personal financial objectives and plans with their bankers put themselves in a good position to prove their worth as good credit risks. Another way to maintain good banking relations is to send information on your financial status and plans to your banker at least periodically. Demonstrating that you are in control of your financial situation gives you an advantage in securing ongoing bank credit.

Warning Signs of Credit Problems

You can prevent serious credit problems by recognizing the early warning signs. If you find *any* of the following happening to you, take action immediately to regain control of your debt.

- You use savings or credit to meet normal household expenses.
- Your credit cards are always at their limits.
- You always make the minimum payments, but your credit card balances are rising each month.
- You start falling behind on important monthly payments, like rent, the mortgage, or a car loan.
- You use one form of credit to make payments on another.
- You are spending more than one-quarter of your after-tax pay on installment debt (not including your mortgage).
- You can't name all your creditors or cite the total amounts you owe them.
- You routinely go to more expensive restaurants and stores because they accept credit cards and you are short of cash.

If you have many debts from different sources, and you aren't sure that you will be able to pay them all, work out a plan for paying the most important bills and for avoiding late charges on all your debts. This entails figuring out just how much it will cost you in terms of interest, late charges, and the possible jeopardy to your credit rating of not paying off each bill in its entirety. For example, one bill might have a minimum balance that will avoid late charges altogether but subject the remaining balance to extraordinarily high interest rates. Missing another bill might expose you to a car repossession or the cutting off of a household utility. Avoid these extremes at all costs. It is extremely hard to reestablish a good credit rating after a repossession, and in the case of a utility, you'll have to pay the bill and any penalties in their entirety, *plus* a start-up charge to have the service reinstated. It is far better to incur additional interest and keep all the accounts active. Beyond minimum payments, pay off the bills with the highest interest rates, like credit cards, first, and then pay any money you can spare toward other debts. If you find that you are one of the many millions of Americans whose debt situation is getting out of control, refer to Chapter Nine, which discusses regaining control over your debts, and Chapter Twenty-one, which covers dealing with anxious creditors.

Credit Bureaus and Your Credit Rating

Although most people have a basic idea of their credit rating, few ever request a copy of their credit bureau report, which lenders use to determine whether an individual is a good credit risk. But you can ask to see that report, and you should. Far better that you should discover a mistake on a routine examination than that a prospective lender should turn you down because of an erroneous report just when you really need a loan.

How to get your credit report. There are thousands of credit bureaus across the country; almost every city and town has at least one. To find out which one has your credit history, ask a banker or retailer with whom you have an account. The Fair Credit Reporting Act requires credit reporting agencies to provide you with a copy or summary of your report upon request. They'll usually mail you a copy, but a few will require you to review it at their office. If, within the last thirty days, you have been turned down for credit because of information contained in the report, you will be allowed to review it free. Otherwise, there probably will be a slight charge.

What you will find. In your credit report you can expect to find:

- Information on your outstanding debts, including balances due on automobile loans, lines of credit, bank credit cards, government-backed student loans, and small business loans.
- A record of how promptly you pay your bills, either by recording recent payments or by a grade assigned you by the creditor.

The report may also contain any of the following.

- The name of your employer.
- Your salary.
- Information from public court records, including bankruptcy filings, legal judgments, tax liens, and divorce settlements.

What you will not find. You will not find any overall judgment of your creditworthiness. That is left up to the people or institutions to whom you apply for credit. Also, not all creditors report to credit bureaus, so all your accounts may not be listed. Credit reports do not contain information on checking or savings accounts, criminal records, race, sex, religion, or personal habits.

If you find a mistake. Chances are you won't find a mistake in your credit report, but if you do, the law provides recourse. If you report a mistake, the credit bureau must investigate. If it finds that you are in the right, it is obliged to notify creditors. If the bureau disputes your claim, you can write a brief statement that will be added to the report. At the very least, this will demonstrate to creditors that you care about your credit.

TO ESTABLISH OR MAINTAIN GOOD CREDIT

- ☐ Establish your creditworthiness by managing your credit wisely.
- ☐ Don't be frustrated by loan rejections. Work to prove that you are a good credit risk.
- ☐ Borrow only for appropriate reasons, and pay off the debt within a reasonable amount of time.
- ☐ Pay at least the minimum amounts due on all bills to avoid late charges.
- ☐ If you have bank loans, keep your bank loan officer up to date on your financial status.
- ☐ If you are ever unable to make a loan payment, contact the lender before they contact you, to work out a payment arrangement.
- ☐ Don't borrow money to finance anything that will be used up quickly or that you don't get any real benefit from.
- ☐ Get out of the habit of always having a car loan.
- ☐ Ask to see your credit report, and have any mistakes corrected.

9

GETTING YOUR DEBTS UNDER CONTROL

I think it's about time I start reducing my debts, rather than seeing them creep up every month. It's not that there's a problem or anything, although the amounts I pay on the credit card loans seem to be increasing. If this economy gets any worse, the last thing I want to have are a lot of debts to worry about.

Reviewing your loans and getting your debts under control are always good ideas, but in the face of what may be a long economic slowdown, it is doubly important. At a minimum, you don't want your debts to get out of control. Ideally, you can work to reduce them so that you will be better prepared for any burdens this recession may dish out to you. The following checklist will help you evaluate your current debt situation and plan to take better control of your indebtedness.

Find out what you owe. The following work sheet will help you summarize your current loans. Don't forget to include all of them. People have a tendency to forget some of their obligations—especially their credit card debt.

SUMMARY OF LOANS

	Amount Owed	Montly Payment
Mortgage	$	$
Home equity loan or second mortgage		
Car loan		
Credit card and charge account loans		
Student loans		
Insurance policy loans		
Other loans		
	$	
	$	

Determine where you stand. Once you have summarized your loans, you may want to figure out where you stand in relation to various guidelines that indicate whether you have or are approaching a debt level that is too high. Two such guidelines follow.

1. Exclusive of your home mortgage or rent, the total amount of your installment debt should be not more than 20 percent of your yearly after-tax income, and not more than one-third of your discretionary income for one year—in other words, the amount you have left over after housing, food, clothing, and taxes.

2. Another sign that you may be approaching a debt level that is too high is if you are unable to save regularly or you find that the amount you are able to save on a regular basis is decreasing.

Stop adding to your debt. Once you find out how much you owe, you need to do two things. First, promise yourself that you will not increase any of your current loan balances. Second, keep your promise. This is a two-step process because it's easy to make these kinds of commitments to yourself, but it's a lot harder to keep them—particularly when you look around at all the conspicuous consumption.

It's easy to get into the debt trap when, over the past several years, you've been able to rely on a steadily rising income to meet steadily rising loan payments. However, many people are about to enter a period where they won't be able to rely on raises every year to meet rising living expenses. If so, something has to give, and all too often it means falling behind on loan payments or worse. So don't complicate matters any more than they are now by adding to your debt.

Prepare a plan to reduce your debts. If you have read this far without casting your eyes away from these pages in dismay, you are ready to prepare a plan to reduce your loans. The following work sheet will help you prepare your plan.

ONE-YEAR PLAN TO REDUCE LOANS

Name of Creditor	Current Balance	Planned Reduction In Loan Balance
_____	$_____	$_____
_____	_____	_____
_____	_____	_____
_____	_____	_____
_____	_____	_____

Plan to reduce the *highest interest rate* loans first. For example, you wouldn't want to reduce your 11 percent automobile loan before reducing your credit card loans at 18 percent interest. Beginning in 1991, there's no tax deduction for consumer debt, so people have lost that excuse to keep loan balances high, hopefully forever. I am always amused by people who believed that it was okay to have many loans because the interest was tax deductible. I wonder if they realize how silly that statement is. For example, if you pay

$1,000 in interest on your home mortgage (which still is fully tax deductible unless you are lucky enough to have a mortgage that's over $1,000,000), and you are in the 28 percent tax bracket, you are going to save $280 in taxes. If you think it's such a good deal to pay somebody $1,000 in order to get $280 back, give me $1,000, and I would be happy to give you $280 in return.

It won't be easy reducing your debts, particularly in 1991. But as you struggle to do so, think about a time when you will be free of all these annoying obligations to credit card companies and automobile companies. If you can discipline yourself by devoting a year, at least, to paying off old debts and adding no new ones, you will like the feeling.

Balance the need to save with the need to reduce your debts. Chances are, if you have managed to accumulate quite a few annoying loans, you haven't been too diligent on the savings side of the equation. If so, you have to leave enough room in your loan reduction plan to allow for increasing your savings at the same time. As we head into tough economic times, you not only will need to get your debts under better control, but you also will have to build up your savings in the event you suffer any financial reversals during the recession. Therefore, you have a formidable but essential challenge ahead of you, which may require some significant reductions in your spending. See Chapter Six for some tips on reducing your expenses.

Some people may have some savings and investments set aside, while at the same time they have let loans creep up. The issue they must address is whether they should use their savings to reduce some of the loans. It makes good financial sense to pay off high-interest rate loans with savings that are almost certainly not earning anywhere near the high interest rates being paid on the loans. However, in view of the tough times ahead, don't deplete your savings in order to pay off loans. It's better to keep some emergency funds set aside in order to meet any unexpected needs during the future difficult economic times.

You really have two choices if you find that your loans are beginning to approach an uncomfortable level. You can wait for hardship to strike, when it will be doubly difficult to get out from under your indebtedness—or you can start now. I think you know which course is preferable. More information on managing your credit is provided in Chapters Eight and Twenty-one.

TO GET YOUR DEBTS UNDER CONTROL

☐ Find out what you owe by preparing a summary of all current loans.

☐ Stop adding to your debt immediately. There is no sense trying to reduce loans with one hand if you are adding to them with the other hand.

☐ Prepare a one-year plan to reduce your debt to a more comfortable level.

☐ Don't devote all your spare resources to reducing debt. It is also necessary to build and maintain a sufficient cash reserve to provide for the unexpected.

10

INSURING THAT YOU ALWAYS HAVE ADEQUATE INSURANCE

This recession is really taking a toll on our finances. We are having so much trouble making ends meet, and we just got two whopping bills for life insurance and house insurance. I think we will let these policies slide so we can have some breathing room.

Suffering uninsured losses is bad enough during good times, but during tough economic times, it is even worse. Unfortunately, when people find their finances pinched, they are tempted to drop some of their insurance coverage. They know they are taking a chance, but tough times call for tough actions. Insurance, however, should be the *last* thing you drop. Adequate insurance coverage is essential to assure your long-term financial well-being: a single gap in your insurance coverage could jeopardize a lifetime's worth of sacrifice and savings. If you are confronted with having to make tough choices in your financial life, don't let insurance be a victim. You might think that if you don't have much in the way of assets, you really don't have much to lose by being uninsured. This is not true. Many people who incur medical bills, are sued, or suffer other losses and are not insured, end up having to pay out of their future earnings.

This chapter will focus on essential areas of insurance coverage. If you are pinched financially, I will show you ways to reduce your insurance premiums to a more affordable level while maintaining the coverage that you need.

Essential Insurance Coverage

The following table lists and describes important areas of insurance coverage.

Type of Insurance	Description/Features
Health Insurance	Protects you from the out-of-pocket costs of health care, and from large cash outflows during major illness.
Homeowner's Insurance	Insures against the theft or destruction of property, such as a home, other structures, personal property, and general contents of the dwelling; protects against the possibility of cash outflows for replacement of these assets.
Renter's Insurance	Protects the personal possessions of the tenant against theft or destruction.
Automobile Insurance	Protects you from large cash outflows for damages resulting from automobile accident or theft.
Extended Personal Liability (Umbrella) Insurance	Protects you from having personal assets or future earnings forfeited as a result of a personal liability suit. Provides additional protection on top of homeowner's/renter's and automobile liability coverage.
Disability Insurance	Replaces part or most of your wage income if you are disabled.

| Life Insurance | Replaces part or most of your wage income in the event of your death, and covers nonrecurring expenses of your dependents during a readjustment period after death. |

Before we get into ways in which you can save money on insurance coverage, the following suggestions will help you make sure you have the correct kind of coverage.

Tips on Acquiring the Right Kind of Insurance Coverage

Health Insurance. Everyone understands the importance of adequate and continuous medical insurance. But you should be aware that policies vary in what they do and do not cover. Generally, this is the one area of insurance where you want to go first-class. Avoid policies that impose a lot of limitations. If you think you might lose your job, know your rights under the law to continue the insurance coverage offered by your former employer at your own expense. Check with the person or department who is responsible for your employer's health benefits, to obtain more details.

Homeowner's/Renter's Insurance. Surprisingly, fewer than one in four renters has renter's insurance, although every renter should. Whether you have homeowner's or renter's insurance, you need to understand the limitations of the standard property insurance policy. Even if you have a comprehensive basic homeowner's or renter's policy, you may not be covered for all of the risks that you want to protect against. You probably need some "optional extras" to obtain the coverage you need. If you are a homeowner, you should be sure your insurance will cover the cost of replacing your home, including any improvements, and allowing for annual inflation. Whether you own your home or rent, replacement cost coverage on your furniture and other personal property is an extremely valuable option. Otherwise, you will be paid actual cash (in other words, depreciated) value for any losses. Replacement cost coverage generally will pay for new replacements of lost items.

Basic homeowner's and renter's policies impose severe limits on the amount that they will pay for lost, stolen, or destroyed valuables. Therefore, if you own any valuables, you should have them professionally appraised and covered under a so-called "floater policy." A floater provides a specific amount of insurance for each object on an itemized basis, guaranteeing full replacement value and eliminating deductibles. Finally, if you store any valuables in a safe-deposit box, you should also obtain a floater that covers these items, since banks rarely provide insurance against losses in safe-deposit boxes.

Extended Personal Liability Insurance. Extended personal liability insurance, also called umbrella insurance, is one of the most often overlooked gaps in insurance coverage. If you don't have this coverage, you are jeopardizing assets that you currently own and perhaps even some of your future earnings. Umbrella policies typically protect you and your family from claims arising out of your personal (not job-related) activities, including legal defense costs. Examples of cases where umbrella insurance comes in handy include a judgment against you for a car accident that exceeds your automobile liability insurance coverage or for any accident that doesn't occur in your car or home. As you are probably aware, we are a lawsuit-crazy country, so it is important for you to secure this protection. Umbrella insurance is coordinated with your automobile and homeowner's or renter's insurance policies, so it is best to acquire it through the company that handles these coverages for you. It is possible that you also may need professional liability insurance if your full-time or part-time job warrants it. If you are unsure, check with an insurance agent who is experienced in professional liability coverage.

Disability Insurance. Disability income insurance is essential for all working people. You are far more likely to suffer from a long-term disability during your working years than you are to die. Usually this insurance is provided by your employer, although you may find that you need to augment it with additional disability insurance that you purchase yourself. Generally, long-term disability coverage should replace 60 to 70 percent of your salary income. Caution: Be wary of how the insurer defines "disability." The best policies will continue disability as long as you suffer a loss of income. Many policies, however, tighten the requirements, so you may not be entitled to benefits if you can work at all, even though you are earning lower wages than you were prior to your disability.

Since these policies are designed to replace a loss of income, if you are unemployed, you cannot obtain disability insurance coverage because you have no income from employment. However, if you become disabled during a period of unemployment, you may be entitled to Social Security benefits, depending upon the extent and duration of your disability. Check with the local Social Security office.

Life Insurance. The primary goal of life insurance is to provide adequate resources for any loved ones who are dependent upon your income in the event of your death. If you are confused about the complexities involved in selecting life insurance, you're not alone. The life insurance industry seems to thrive on confusion. If you have no dependents, the life insurance provided by your employer may be sufficient. People with dependent children need a lot of life insurance. But children aren't necessarily the only dependents that you might have. For example, "dinks," dual income couples with no kids, may need more life insurance than they think if, as is often the case, their lifestyle is such that a surviving spouse would be financially crippled by the other's demise.

Figuring out how much life insurance you need is no easy task. Often, those who are most anxious to tell you how much you need are those who want to sell you a lot of expensive insurance. Generally speaking, the minimum amount of life insurance you should have is enough to get the family back on a firm economic footing in the event of your death. You may want more, but I don't think you need so much that your family could retire in the lap of luxury if you died.

Tips on Reducing Your Insurance Costs

Insurance premiums for many types of coverage have skyrocketed in recent years. Yet most people pay more than they have to for insurance coverage. There are two ways to reduce your insurance costs. First, you or your agent should shop around for the best premium prices. The insurance industry is very price-competitive these days, and people have told me numerous times that by taking a little initiative, or prodding their agents to take some initiative, they have been able to save hundreds of dollars on their annual insurance costs. Second, make sure you pay only for the policy features and options you need. All too often, people purchase a "Rolls-Royce" policy when an "Oldsmobile" would suit them just fine.

The following suggestions will help you save some insurance money at a time when you could probably use the money for other worthwhile purposes. One of the few good things to come out of bad economic times is that we are forced—out of fear, if not financial necessity—to become wiser consumers. I hope that you will carry these good habits, including being a wiser insurance consumer, forward when prosperity returns anew.

Health Insurance. If you are fortunate enough to have your health insurance provided, or more likely, subsidized by your employer, be sure you understand what it does and doesn't provide. You may be offered a choice of plans, each of which offers different types of coverage. Many people, realizing that they shouldn't skimp on health insurance, automatically select the policy that costs the most. Instead, you should select the policy that provides the kind of coverage that you and your family need—and it may not be the most expensive policy.

- If both you and your spouse work for companies that subsidize employees' health insurance, compare what each company offers before deciding how to arrange your medical coverage. By doing so, you may be able to save some money.
- If you have to buy health insurance on your own, it is almost always cheaper to do so as a member of a group rather than as an individual. Chances are that you can join a professional organization or other local groups, such as the Chamber of Commerce, that offer group health insurance to its members.

Homeowner's/Renter's Insurance. There are a few ways to reduce your homeowner's or renter's insurance premium without affecting the coverage that you need.

- Obtain quotes from a variety of insurance companies. In the past few years, many people have been delighted to learn how much they can save by changing from the insurer they had been with for years to another insurer. Savings of 50 percent or more are possible in some instances, in this highly competitive industry. When you shop around, obtain quotes only from larger, financially strong insurers (those rated "A" or better by A.M. Best, the insurance rating organization), since the insurance industry is going through a recession too.

- Whatever company you choose, ask them how you can reduce your premium. For example, taking measures to improve home security may result in a premium reduction, although, of course, you will have to incur the upfront cost in order to receive the premium reduction.

- Many people select a low deductible on their homeowner's or renter's insurance without thinking. If you have a bit of a financial cushion—in other words, if you can afford to pay, say, the first $1,000 of a loss—select a higher deductible and save some premium dollars. Hopefully, you are on that happy bandwagon already. If not, I hope you will be able to jump on it soon.

Automobile Insurance. Ways to reduce auto insurance premiums abound.

- Increasing the deductible on your collision coverage to $500 from $200 could reduce your collision insurance cost by 15 to 30 percent. You may want to consider dropping your collision coverage or comprehensive coverage if you drive an old car, as I do.

- You may be able to eliminate some of the medical coverage on your auto policy if it duplicates coverage you already have on your health-insurance policy.

- The total cost of insurance is affected by the type of car you drive. Buying a "low-profile" car, one that's less costly to repair and less attractive to thieves, will save you premium dollars. It will also save you money when you buy the car in the first place.
- Check with your insurance agent to see what other discounts are available. Many are beginning to expand the array of discounts offered, including ones for cars with air bags, automatic seat belts, antilock brakes, and antitheft devices. Discounts also may be available for students with good grades, drivers over fifty, and of course, clean driving records.

Disability Insurance. Disability income insurance provided by your employer may or may not be sufficient to meet your needs in terms of policy provisions and extent of coverage. If you have to purchase this absolutely essential coverage individually, the following suggestions may save you some money.

- Similar to health insurance, many professional organizations and affinity groups provide disability insurance coverage for their members that is much cheaper than individually purchased policies.
- If you do purchase an individual policy, you'll be surprised at how expensive it is. Disability policies have more options than most new cars. Some may be worthwhile, such as cost-of-living adjustments for benefits, but don't buy any bells and whistles you don't need.
- Finally, one way to save on disability premiums is to extend the waiting period—in other words, the time between the onset of your disability and when benefits commence. Policies with short waiting periods, say thirty days, are much more expen-

sive than those with longer waiting periods, say six months or even one year. If you think you can get by for a few months when you are disabled, you can save quite a bit of premium money by opting for a longer waiting period.

Life Insurance. When economic times get tough, many people see dropping some or all of their life insurance coverage as an easy way to cut expenses. Instead of reducing your coverage and jeopardizing your family's security, try to make the most of your life insurance dollar by heeding the following suggestions.

• Some people have too much life insurance. If so, they obviously can save money by dropping unnecessary coverage. Your life insurance needs change, and in some instances decline, particularly as you age and children leave the nest. Review your coverage periodically to assure that you have an appropriate amount.

• There are plenty of ways to buy low-cost life insurance coverage, if you devote some time to it. Believe me, it will be time well spent, because identical life insurance policies vary dramatically in price. Why pay more for something as dull as life insurance? First, your employer may offer you the option of buying additional coverage, usually at low group rates. Next, professional associations and groups offer low-cost group term coverage. If you are a resident of or work in Connecticut, Massachusetts, or New York, check the rates on savings bank life insurance. Finally, if you purchase your own insurance, either directly or through an agent, compare the rates of several companies. As with all insurance, purchase only from financially strong insurers: Insurance experts expect that some weaker companies may experience severe financial difficulties during the recession.

- It generally is unwise to let a cash-value policy that you've owned for several years lapse in favor of cheaper insurance. Inquire instead as to whether you can lower or eliminate your premium payments (by using the cash value to pay the premiums) while continuing the coverage.
- If possible, pay your life insurance premium annually. If you pay in installments, your total cost will be higher.
- Never buy credit life insurance on an installment loan, auto loan, mortgage loan, or any loan. Credit life insurance will pay off your loan if you die while the loan is outstanding. This insurance is, almost without exception, horrendously expensive, and don't be misled into thinking that it is a condition of granting the loan. If that is implied, chances are that the lender is breaking the law.

IN ORDER TO MAKE THE MOST OF YOUR INSURANCE DOLLAR

Be sure you have adequate coverage in each of the following areas.

- [ ] Health insurance
- [ ] Homeowner's or Renter's insurance
- [ ] Automobile insurance
- [ ] Extended personal liability (umbrella) insurance
- [ ] Disability insurance
- [ ] Life insurance

Continuing your insurance coverage must be a high priority item in your budget. If you are experiencing financial stress, don't be tempted to let this vital coverge lapse.

Look for ways to reduce your insurance costs in each area of coverage. With a moderate amount of effort, you may be able to save hundreds of dollars.

PART

III

INVESTING IN TOUGH ECONOMIC TIMES

11

INVESTMENT STRATEGIES FOR FRIGHTENED INVESTORS

I have no idea how to invest in a recession. The last time we had a recession, I had no investments to worry about. I don't have a whole lot now, but I don't want to make any big mistakes with my hard-earned money.

In 1991 it will not be easy to invest. No matter how much or how little you have to invest, you probably have been tempted in recent months to sell all your investments and put your money in the safest possible securities. If you are very frightened and preoccupied about losing money on your investments, it could make sense, for your own peace of mind, to "go into cash," as Wall Street says. But there is a danger in taking this course, just as there is a danger in, say, putting all your money into stocks in 1991. The problem with being overly conservative is that, over the long run, your investments won't grow nearly as much as they would if you had some other, admittedly riskier, securities in your investment portfolio. On the other hand, the danger of putting all your eggs into the "stock basket" is that stocks do sometimes decline in value, as occurred in 1990. Investors who had all or most of their money in stocks in 1990 are obviously poorer on paper, at least, than they would have been had they spread their money into other kinds of investments.

In this chapter you will learn ways to structure your investments so that you can invest wisely during 1991 without losing sleep. Depending on your outlook, I will show you several ways to invest. You may be optimistic about the prospects for stocks and bonds during 1991. Perhaps you are pessimistic; you have every reason to be. But most likely you, like most people, have no idea what is going to happen. You want to invest so that you can take advantage of a market rebound if and when it occurs, yet you want some protection against market adversity as well.

Before I get into specific investment strategies, I'll explain in this chapter about investment categories and "investment allocation," which means deciding how much of your money you will invest in each of the various investment categories. Investment allocation is not difficult to understand, and it is important to your long-term investment success.

This chapter is the first in a series of investment chapters. It forms a foundation that will help you understand the information that follows. Chapter Twelve contains ten rules for investing successfully during tough times. Chapter Sixteen lists some stocks and mutual funds that should give you comfort during 1991 and beyond. Finally, Chapters Thirteen, Fourteen, and Fifteen offer tips for making the right stock, interest-earning, and real estate investments during this rough economic climate. One final note: These chapters don't assume that you have ten million dollars to invest. The information provided should help you, even if you're just starting out building your savings and investments.

Investment Categories

Saving regularly and investing those savings wisely are the two most important things you can do to meet major financial obligations during your lifetime, cope with financial emergencies that may occur as a result of this recession or future adversity, and ultimately, achieve financial security. As you will find in this chapter and the following investment chapters, it's not that difficult to be a good investor—one who can make sensible investment decisions on his or her own.

There are three major categories of investments.

1. **Stock investments** can be purchased by buying individual shares directly or by buying stock mutual funds. See Chapter Thirteen.

2. **Interest-earning investments** can be purchased directly or through interest-earning mutual funds. Interest-earning investments are typically divided into two subcategories: *cash equivalent investments,* which are interest-earning securities that can readily be turned into cash with little or no change in principal value, and *fixed-income investments,* which are longer-term securities whose value can fluctuate depending upon changes in prevailing interest rates. See Chapter Fourteen.

3. **Real estate investments** can be purchased and managed directly, or indirectly, through real estate limited partnerships or real estate investment trusts. The following discussion on investment allocation will consider only interest-earning investments and stocks, since most people choose not to invest in real estate (except for their own home). If you currently invest or are considering investing in real estate, see Chapter Fifteen.

Investment Allocation

Investment allocation means deciding how much of your investment portfolio, however large or small it might be, should be invested in stocks and how much should be in the two categories of interest-earning investments, fixed-income and cash equivalent. All too often investors tend to invest in extremes, placing too much emphasis on a single investment category. Even though they may think they are investing wisely, they are probably overlooking other investments that would help them achieve investment success. At this point, it might be useful for you to summarize your current investment allocation, to find out how your investments are divvied up. Use the work sheet below. If you need some help distinguishing between cash equivalent and fixed-income investments, refer to Chapter Fourteen.

Why allocate your investments? First, investors tend to focus too much on the short term under any circumstances, and even more so during uncertain economic times. It's the long-term view that is the least risky, though, and over the long term, a well-balanced allocation of investments will produce the best return with a reasonable level of risk. Second, a common response to scary investment markets is to put most or all of your money into cash equivalents.

MY CURRENT INVESTMENT ALLOCATION

Investment Category	$ Value	% of Total Portfolio
Cash equivalents	$_____	$_____%
Fixed-income securities	_____	_____
Stocks	_____	_____
Total	$_____	100%

Although this may be the place to be if the stock market kept dropping forever, the truth is, as will be explained in later chapters, stock market rebounds usually begin before a recession is over. Missing these often fast rebounds will almost certainly drag down long-term performance. This is not to say that investors should necessarily be going into stocks in a big way, either. What's important is striking a balance among stocks, fixed-income investments, and cash equivalents.

Over the long run, a commonly accepted investment allocation is in the range of a 50–50 split between stocks and interest-earning securities, although people who are retired or are nearing retirement age should increase their allocation of safer, interest-earning securities. During trying times like these, many investors feel more comfortable reducing the proportion they have invested in stocks, and the sample 1991 investment allocations outlined below do just that. This is fine, but if you feel that you have too much invested in stock, you should shift out gradually. No matter how bad or good you might think conditions are, avoid any rapid redeployment of your investments. Investors who shift into and out of stocks and other investments frequently almost inevitably end up doing the wrong thing at the wrong time.

A Word About Stocks

To illustrate the importance of having stocks in a portfolio, consider the performance of stocks compared with cash equivalents from 1960 to 1989. Cash-equivalent investments, as measured by the performance of Treasury bills, returned a compound annual rate of 6.3 percent. Stocks, as measured by the performance of the Standard & Poor's 500 stock index, provided a 10.3 percent compound annual rate of return. There certainly were years between 1960 and 1989 when stocks went down in price, just as in 1990. Which years? 1962, 1966, 1969, 1973, 1974, 1977, and 1981. While the difference between a 6.3 percent return on cash equivalents and 10.3 percent return on stocks may not seem so great, it really is. If you had invested $10,000 in Treasury bills alone in 1960, excluding taxes paid on the interest, you would have had almost $63,000 in the till as of the end of 1989. If the $10,000 had been put in stocks, assuming the stocks performed like the S&P 500 index and before considering the effect of income taxes, you would have had over $189,000, or three times what you would have had in Treasury bills.

Three Investment Forecasts for 1991

It is impossible to predict what is actually going to happen in the investment markets in 1991. It's particularly difficult in light of the many uncertainties facing the U.S. economy, as described in Chapter One. But before you can decide how your money should be invested in 1991, you have to form at least a tentative outlook on market performance. To help you, three different forecasts are presented below, reflecting negative, neutral, and positive scenarios for investment performance in 1991. Each forecast includes its own investment allocation, and following that are suggested portfolios for each forecast.

Forecast 1: "The sky is falling."

Do you believe that the economy is headed for a shellacking? If so, you may want to avoid stocks and fixed-income investments in favor of safe, stable, cash-equivalent investments. You also might prefer this investment scenario if you don't want to risk any possible loss in your investments next year—perhaps you are saving for a house or some other big-ticket item.

A possible investment allocation under "the sky is falling" forecast could be: 60 percent cash-equivalent investments; 20 percent fixed-income investments; and 20 percent stock investments. Of course, very pessimistic investors could move even more of their money into cash-equivalent investments—how much depends on the strength of their convictions that the sky is indeed falling in. These investors also must weigh the effects, not the least of which are transaction costs and possible tax consequences, of moving their investments into an all- or nearly all-cash position. Generally, as discussed in Chapter Twelve, it is unwise to make precipitous shifts in your investments in response to anticipated, but of course unknown, market conditions.

Forecast 2: "Up and down the market goes; where it stops nobody knows."

This neutral forecast is probably shared by many people. It reflects a commonly held view: "I simply don't know what's going to happen to the investment markets in 1991." The investment allocation under this forecast reflects a somewhat cautious approach, but it still is more aggressive than the previous, pessimistic forecast. It has a heavier weighting of stocks and fixed-income investments than does Forecast 1. If you are really uncertain about market conditions in 1991, but are not afraid that the sky is going to fall in, this forecast may be right for you. A possible neutral investment allocation is: 30 percent cash-equivalent investments; 35 percent fixed-income investments; and 35 percent stock investments.

Forecast 3: "Opportunity knocks with bonds and stocks."

Some investors, and you may be one of them, think that 1991 will be a year of real investment opportunity. Stocks may rebound after the slaughter of 1990, and interest rates may come down as the recession progresses. These optimists think that there is nothing to be gained by hiding behind cash-equivalent investments, and everything to be gained by taking some risks. Proponents of Forecast 3 take the classic contrarian view. The experts think that the markets are going to stink in 1991; therefore, they believe that stocks and bonds will perform superbly. The following is a possible investment allocation for the optimistic investor in 1991: 15 percent cash-equivalent investments; 40 percent fixed-income investments; and 45 percent stock investments.

Sample Investment Portfolios

Six sample portfolios appear below. The first three show how you could invest $10,000 under each of the forecasts described above. The last three do the same for a $100,000 portfolio, if you are fortunate enough to have that much money to invest. If you aren't yet in either of these leagues, I then will show you how you can invest $1,000 wisely and well.

Size of your investment portfolio: $10,000
Your investment outlook for 1991: "The sky is falling" (negative)

Suggested portfolio:

Cash Equivalents (60 percent)
    $ 6,000   in safe, cash-equivalent investments

Fixed-income Securities (20 percent)
  $ 2,000   in a government-securities mutual fund

Stocks (20 percent)
  $ 2,000   in a growth-and-income mutual fund

  $10,000   total portfolio

Size of your investment portfolio: $10,000
Your investment outlook for 1991: "Up & down . . ." (neutral)

Suggested portfolio:

Cash Equivalents (30 percent)
  $ 3,000   in safe, cash-equivalent investments

Fixed-income Securities (35 percent)
  $ 1,500   in a high-quality corporate bond fund
    2,000   in a government-securities mutual fund
    3,500   total fixed-income investments

Stocks (35 percent)
  $ 2,500   in a growth-and-income mutual fund
    1,000   in an international stock mutual fund
    3,500   total stock investments

  $10,000   total portfolio

Size of your investment portfolio: $10,000
Your investment outlook for 1991: "Opportunity knocks . . ."
(positive)

Suggested portfolio:

Cash Equivalents (15 percent)
$ 1,500   in safe, cash-equivalent investments

Fixed-income Securities (40 percent)
$ 2,000   in a high-quality corporate bond mutual fund
  2,000   in a government-securities mutual fund
  4,000   total fixed-income investments

Stocks (45 percent)
$ 1,000   in a maximum-capital-gains mutual fund
  2,500   in a growth-and-income mutual fund
  1,000   in an international stock mutual fund
  4,500   total stock investments

$10,000   total portfolio

Size of your investment portfolio: $100,000
Your investment outlook for 1991: "The sky is falling" (negative)

Suggested portfolio:

Cash Equivalents (60 percent)
$ 60,000   in safe, cash-equivalent investments

Fixed-income Securities (20 percent)
$ 10,000   in high-quality municipal or corporate bonds or
           Treasury securities
  10,000   in a government-securities mutual fund
  20,000   total fixed-income investments

Stocks (20 percent)
$ 15,000   in a growth-and-income mutual fund
   5,000   in an international stock mutual fund
  20,000   total stock investments

$100,000   total portfolio

Size of your investment portfolio: $100,000
Your investment outlook for 1991: "Up & down . . ." (neutral)

Suggested portfolio:

Cash Equivalents (30 percent)
$ 30,000   in safe, cash-equivalent investments

Fixed-income Securities (35 percent)
$ 20,000   in high-quality municipal or corporate bonds or
          Treasury securities
  10,000   in a government-securities mutual fund
   5,000   in a municipal-bond mutual fund
  35,000   total fixed-income investments

Stocks (35 percent)
$ 15,000 $5,000 in each of three high-quality stocks
   5,000   in a maximum-capital-gains mutual fund
  10,000   in a growth-and-income mutual fund
   5,000   in an international stock mutual fund
  35,000   total stock investments

$100,000   total portfolio

Size of your investment portfolio: $100,000
Your investment outlook for 1991: "Opportunity knocks . . ."
(positive)

Suggested portfolio:

Cash Equivalents (15 percent)
$ 15,000   in safe, cash-equivalent investments

Fixed-income Securities (40 percent)
$ 20,000   in high-quality municipal or corporate bonds or
           Treasury securities
   5,000   in a corporate-bond mutual fund
  10,000   in a government-securities mutual fund
   5,000   in a municipal-bond mutual fund
  40,000   total fixed-income investments

Stocks (45 percent)
$ 20,000 $5,000 in each of four high-quality stocks
  10,000   in a maximum-capital-gains mutual fund
  10,000   in a growth-and-income mutual fund
   5,000   in an international stock mutual fund
  45,000   total stock investments

$100,000   total portfolio

Please note that the portfolios suggested above are
only illustrations of the many possible ways you can
invest wisely and well. Part of the fun of investing is
to build a portfolio that meets your outlook for the
market as well as your personal objectives.

The $1,000 Portfolio

As I said earlier, you can invest even relatively small
amounts of money, $1,000 or less, and still achieve

diversification and professional balance. How? By investing in any of the many mutual funds that accept low initial investments. Some, including the venerable Twentieth Century Funds (telephone 800-345-2021) have no minimum initial investment requirements. Moreover, you can combine stocks, fixed-income investments, and cash equivalent investments in a single mutual fund, a so-called balanced fund. Some good ones are listed in Chapter Sixteen.

Defensive Investment Strategies

You will hear a lot about defensive investing during 1991. Defensive investing emphasizes the avoidance of serious mistakes or losses by concentrating on investments that are thought to be resistant to significant loss. When investment market conditions are particularly uncertain or adverse, many investors prefer defensive investments. I'm not going to go into great detail here, because defensive investing is what Part III of this book is all about, but here's a brief overview.

In the stock arena, defensive investors opt for high-quality stocks in strong, defensive industries. A list of defensive industry groups appears in Chapter Sixteen. A defensive fixed-income investment strategy involves the selection of high-quality fixed-income securities—typically Treasury notes, Treasury bonds, or other fixed-income securities that are highly rated by the rating agencies, namely Standard & Poor's and Moody's. Defensive investors also may prefer shorter-maturity fixed-income investments, which will fluctuate in value less than longer-maturity fixed-income investments in response to changes in prevailing interest rates. A final and often-used defensive investment strategy is to emphasize high-quality cash-equivalent investments for absolute protection of invested funds against loss.

Ten Stable Investments for the Recession-Wary

Do you want absolute or almost absolute protection against loss for all or a portion of your investments? You can't go wrong with any of the following stable cash equivalent investments. Another advantage: If inflation heats up, the interest rates on these securities will, sooner or later, increase as well. The drawback to these investments is that after you pay income taxes on the interest, you'll probably barely beat inflation. But for the truly frightened investor, that may be a worthwhile trade-off during 1991. So select any of these stable investments, and sleep tight. Several of these investments are issued by banks, savings and loans, or credit unions. Be sure to buy only investments that are federally insured.

1. Certificates of deposit
2. Money market deposit accounts
3. Money market mutual funds
4. Municipal notes
5. Savings accounts
6. Single state, tax-exempt money market mutual funds
7. Tax-exempt money market mutual funds
8. Treasury bills
9. U.S. savings bonds
10. U.S. Treasury money market mutual funds

12

TEN RULES FOR INVESTING SUCCESSFULLY IN TURBULENT MARKETS

My investments are a mess, I think. Even though I don't have much in the way of investments, the money is important to me, and sometimes I feel that I should be making some of the moves that the experts suggest. Other times I get so worried that I think about selling everything and putting my money in a savings account. It's tough enough investing when times are good, but who knows what to do in a recession?

This chapter contains ten rules that will help you invest sensibly in a rough and unpredictable economy, whether you have $1,000 or $1,000,000 to invest. I'm not going to suggest that there are great opportunities or secret ways to get rich quick. I'm not going to tell you to do strange things with your money, like put it all in gold coins or ship it overseas. I'm not going to tell you what's going to happen to stock prices, where interest rates are heading, or what's going to happen in the real estate market. I don't know how these investments will perform in 1991, and neither does anyone else, although some would like you to believe that they do. Instead, I will explain ten straightforward rules for successful investing during a recession.

These rules are probably not going to make you rich in 1991, but they won't make you poor either. Many of the rules can help you invest successfully in any market, but they are *essential* in tough markets. People who get themselves into trouble with their investments during unpredictable and volatile markets inevitably violate one of these rules. Yet, the rules aren't that difficult or time consuming to follow.

1. **Stick to high quality investments.** The recession is starting with an unprecedented number of debt-bloated corporations, banks, real estate firms, states, and municipalities. Heavily indebted businesses are going to have trouble coping with this recession, and many won't survive. It's even possible that some debt-laden states and cities will have difficulty meeting their obligations. Just about every responsible observer of the 1991 investment scene echoes one consistent theme—investors need to emphasize quality above all else in their investments. Investment quality has always been important in surviving recessions, and it's crucially important in this one. In short, a high-quality investment is one that has the ability to survive, and perhaps even thrive, during the harshest economic conditions.

You should not only purchase high-quality investments in 1991 but also review the investments you already own, to be sure that they can weather the economic downturn. Chapters Thirteen, Fourteen, and Fifteen discuss quality considerations in stocks, interest-earning investments, and real estate, while Chapter Sixteen lists some high-quality stocks and mutual funds.

2. **Balance your investments.** Whether your invest-

ment portfolio is small or large, it should be balanced, consisting of appropriate proportions of stock investments and interest-earning investments. For example, you might decide that an appropriate allocation would be 50 percent stocks and 50 percent interest-earning investments, or 30 percent stocks and 70 percent interest-earning investments. If you also invest in real estate, your portfolio should consist of appropriate proportions of stocks, interest-earning investments, and real estate. (See Chapter Eleven.)

3. **Take a long term view.** Successful investors are patient and disciplined. They decide how to allocate their investments between stocks and interest-earning securities, and they don't vary those proportions significantly. They only make investments with the intention of holding them for many years. Most importantly, they don't overreact to current market conditions by shifting their investments hither and yon.

Recessions create exceedingly tough investment environments. Stock and real estate prices often weaken, but they may well rebound before the recession is over. Interest rates usually decline, but they could increase. In short, it's virtually impossible to foretell what will happen to your investments, and it is in these times that many investors tend to overreact. When an economist says that stock prices are going to plummet, they turn around and sell most or all of their stocks. Later they reinvest in stocks because another supposed expert states that stock prices are going to go through the roof. Other investors simply react to events, not opinions. Many sold their stocks right after the October 1987 crash, when if anything, they should have been buying. It never pays to suddenly flip-flop your investments, particularly in unpredictable times.

4. **Buy or sell gradually.** Investors who quickly make major changes in their investments almost al-

ways end up worse off than if they had made them
gradually. Whether you are redeploying your portfolio
to achieve better balance and diversification, fine tun-
ing your investment allocations, or deciding how to
invest a recent windfall, do so gradually. For example,
perhaps you are really concerned about the outlook
for stocks. Although you intend to keep some stocks,
you would like to lighten up your holdings. If so, don't
sell everything in one day. Plan to sell gradually,
perhaps over a period of months. Another example:
Say interest rates rise to the point where you find
interest-earning securities particularly attractive, and
you would like to invest. Again, don't commit all your
resources at once. After all, interest rates could rise
even further, and you don't want a lot of your money
stuck in interest-earning securities if rates are still
rising.

One of the best ways to add to your investments
gradually is to use dollar-cost averaging—simply invest a fixed amount on a regular basis. The trick is to
stick with your schedule, regardless of whether stock
or bond prices go up or down. Because you're investing a fixed amount at fixed intervals, your dollars buy
fewer shares when stock or bond prices are high and
more when they are low. As a result, the average
purchase price is lower than the average market price
over the same time frame. You can't beat that. You
can use dollar-cost averaging with individual security
purchases, but it often is easier with stock or bond
mutual funds. While dollar-cost averaging won't dramatically improve the performance of your portfolio,
it does add discipline to your investing and give you
the benefits of saving regularly.

5. **Diversify.** Within each investment category in
your portfolio, the individual investments should be
diversified. Diversification of stock, interest-earning
investments, and if you have them, real estate invest-

ments is essential to your long-term investment success, and it could be one of the most important things you do to ensure investing successfully. Diversification protects us from many mistakes that we make in our investments. We all make investment mistakes, otherwise we would all be billionaires. Recently, many people have become painfully aware of the dangers of not diversifying. You may be one of them. For example, scads of investors were attracted to the high yields offered by junk bonds and junk-bond mutual funds. Sadly, many of them didn't understand the meaning of the word "junk." They probably figured that all bonds are safe, and since a junk bond fund consisted of hundreds of different bonds, they were *very* safe. Of course, high yield means high risk, and many junk-bond investors who placed most of their savings in them have suffered a financial setback. Were they wrong to invest in junk bonds in the first place? Perhaps not, as long as they didn't risk too much of their money in them. A well-diversified portfolio of interest-earning investments might consist of CDs, Treasury securities or Treasury mutual funds, high-quality corporate bonds or bond funds, and perhaps, *some* junk-bond funds. But a substantial portion of your investments should never be in a single type of security.

With respect to stock investments, some people, particularly employees of large corporations, may have too much money tied up in a single stock issue. This is unwise. You need only ask employees of some of the major computer companies or money center banks who loaded up on stock in their companies. Sure, they had a lot of confidence in their company's prospects, but confidence does not mean an ever-increasing stock price. The stock of Digital Equipment Corporation (DEC), for example, declined from a high of $199 per share in 1987 to under $50 per share in November 1990. Employees who purchased a lot of

stock in the Bank of New England fared even worse.
That stock went from $17 per share to $1 per share in
a matter of months.

If you invest in a single-stock mutual fund, you may
think that you are well-diversified. To the extent that
your fund invests in many companies, you are. But it
is also important to diversify across mutual fund categories. For example, many people prefer the most
aggressive "maximum capital gains" stock mutual
funds, which do fabulously well in up markets, but
often perform abysmally in down markets. This is not
the time to have a lot of money tied up in a single
maximum capital gains fund. It's better to spread your
money around and invest in, perhaps, a growth and
income fund and an international fund. That way you
won't suffer as much if the market continues on its
downward course as you would if all of your money
were tied up in a maximum capital gains fund. Growth-
and-income funds invest in higher-quality dividend-
paying stocks, which are better able to withstand
economic downturns than are the more speculative
high-growth stocks that maximum-capital-gains funds
invest in. International funds, of course, invest in
foreign stocks. By investing in all three you can
achieve greater diversification and some protection
against a declining U.S. stock market.

6. **Use mutual funds to help achieve your objectives.**
Surprisingly, three out of four American households
do not invest in mutual funds. Yet mutual funds have
a lot to offer novice and experienced investors alike.
In fact, many of the most successful professional
money managers and the largest pension funds invest
in mutual funds to help achieve their investment objectives. Certainly, you can benefit as well. There are
numerous advantages of mutual funds, not the least of
which are diversification, low management fees, and
professional management. If ever there was a time

when you could benefit from professional management, it's now. Most fund managers have lived through past recessions, and they have enormous resources at their fingertips. What's more, you can get that management expertise with an investment of just a few hundred dollars. There are over two thousand mutual funds, so you should have no trouble finding a fund that fits your needs. If you do your own research, which doesn't take much expertise or time, you can select a no-load fund and avoid paying a commission. Some good no-load funds are listed in Chapter Sixteen. Mutual funds help you avoid much of the inconvenience and worry of purchasing and managing individual investments. You've already got enough to worry about in 1991. Let a mutual fund manager worry about some of your investments.

7. **Take control of your investments.** Taking control of your investments may be the last thing you want to do during a difficult market. What is your alternative? Are you comfortable letting someone else make decisions for you? Most of us don't have enough money to invest to be able to afford individualized money management. Taking control of your investments doesn't mean you should make every investment decision. If it did, I wouldn't speak so highly of mutual funds, because once you select a mutual fund, you have no control over how your money is invested. Taking control of your investments means staying involved. If you rely on someone to recommend investments, fine, but be sure that you understand each investment and decide whether it is appropriate for you. If you develop a sensible, disciplined, and consistent approach to investing, you can be your own best investment manager. Another advantage of taking control of your investments is that it forces you to stay up to date with market conditions and events, so you can take

advantage of market opportunities and anticipate problems.

8. **Follow key indicators.** In order to manage your money more effectively, you need to monitor some measures of investment value. There are two commonly available and widely used measures, one for stock and one for interest-earning investments.

- A readily available measure of relative stock prices is the price-earnings (P/E) ratio of the Dow Jones Industrial Average (DJIA). The P/E ratio of the DJIA is calculated by dividing the total market price of the thirty stocks in the DJIA by the total earnings per share of the thirty stocks. A price-earnings ratio of the DJIA well above its historical average for the DJIA may indicate that stocks are overpriced. For example, the DJIA P/E ratio reached twenty shortly before the October 1987 stock market crash. The average DJIA P/E ratio over the past several years has been about fourteen. You may want to consider the current P/E ratio for the DJIA in deciding whether to invest in stocks. If it's well above the historical average, avoid stocks and stock mutual funds. If below, consider buying. The Dow Jones P/E ratio is available in the *Wall Street Journal* and *Barron's*.

- The yield on the thirty-year Treasury bond is often used as a bellwether to judge how high or low interest rates are. Most interest rates move in tandem with the yield on long-term Treasury securities. In recent years, thirty-year Treasury bond yields around 9 percent have signaled attractive returns from interest-earning investments. Hence, when the long-term Treasury yield approaches or exceeds 9 percent, you may wish to purchase longer-term interest-earning securities— or mutual funds that invest in them—to lock in high interest rates. If you feel that interest rates are low—perhaps under 8 percent—buy shorter-term interest-earning or cash-equivalent investments such as money market funds. (See Chapter Fourteen.) Yields on thirty-year Treasury bonds are commonly available in the financial press.

9. **Stick with old-fashioned investments.** Would you entrust your money to a stranger? Probably not. Why, then, do so many people invest in securities that they don't understand? Isn't that the equivalent of entrusting money to a stranger? It's going to be difficult enough to make money on your investments in 1991. Don't make it even more difficult by investing in the unusual. You may have received a phone call recently from someone offering a new and improved investment that is "perfect for an astute investor like you." The expected annual return on the investment is, of course, staggering. If the investment pans out, you'll be able to retire in Tahiti next year, consigned to a life of splendiferous luxury. Don't believe the hype. Always keep Pond's Rule of You'rebeingbamboozled in mind: "If someone who's trying to sell you an investment can't explain it to your satisfaction in one sentence, don't buy it."

There's nothing wrong with old-fashioned investments, such as blue-chip stocks, high-grade bonds, certificates of deposit, and long-lived mutual funds. You can't brag about them to your cronies, lest they accuse you of being dull. But you can rely on them, and reliability will be very comforting during the current economic malaise. Almost all American families who created a lot of personal wealth through investing did so by buying old-fashioned investments and holding on to them. They lost money during bad economic times, but they more than made up for the losses during prosperous times. They didn't speculate, even though they could afford to. They invested in the same old-fashioned securities in good times and bad. We should all learn a lesson from their success. Next time you're tempted to invest in an adjustable-rate preferred fund or an OEX put option, buy some GE stock instead.

10. **Keep adding to your investments.** Whether you already have a sizable portfolio, are a beginner, or are somewhere in between, the best way to achieve financial security is by adding to your investments regularly. In other words, save and invest, save and invest. One of the easiest ways to increase your investments is to reinvest your dividend, interest, and capital-gains income, rather than spending the checks on something you really don't need. Income from your mutual funds can be automatically reinvested simply by asking the fund company to do so. If you hold dividend-paying stocks, the corporation may have a dividend reinvestment program that not only reinvests your dividends but also permits you to buy additional shares of stock directly from the company at little or no commission.

It is impossible to save too much money, unless you have no money left over for food. To see how regular savings can add up over the years, consider the following examples: Jack has $10,000 sitting in some investments. In twenty years, when he plans to retire, that $10,000 will grow to about $47,000 if he can earn 8 percent on his money. Jeanne also has $10,000 and also expects to earn an 8 percent return. But she plans to add $100 per month in savings to her $10,000 stash. With just $100 per month savings over twenty years plus the $10,000 she has now, Jeanne's investment account will grow to $111,000!

Saving and investing are particularly important today, since we can't predict what this recession will do to us. The more resources you have to fall back on, the better off you will be in the event that you are adversely affected by the recession. If you follow the above rules for investing during tough times, you'll be able to survive—or even flourish—during the recession, and you'll be on your way to profiting handsomely from the prosperity that will follow.

SUCCESSFUL INVESTING IN 1991

☐ Purchase and hold only high-quality investments. This is no time to make risky investments.

☐ Balance your investments by having appropriate amounts of stock investments, interest-earning investments, and perhaps, real estate investments.

☐ Invest for the long term.

☐ Buy or sell your investments gradually. Never make any sudden changes in your investments, even in the current unsettling investment environment.

☐ Diversify your investments by holding a variety of securities within each investment category. If you have few investments, you can achieve diversification with mutual funds at low cost.

☐ Include mutual funds in your portfolio, whether it is large or small, to take advantage of professional management during difficult times.

☐ Take control over your investments, whether you rely on others to advise you or you make your own investment decisions. Don't be overly influenced by others in the current confusing and unpredictable investment climate.

☐ Follow key indicators of market value and prevailing interest rates in order to judge investment values better.

☐ Only make investments that you understand. This is no time to experiment with new or unusual investments, no matter how attractive they appear.

☐ Keep adding to your investments by saving regularly and reinvesting your dividends and interest income. Let the miracle of saving and compounding make you financially secure.

MAKING THE RIGHT STOCK INVESTMENTS DURING TOUGH TIMES

The stock market scares the daylights out of me. My stock investments were way down in 1990. I've read that it's too late to sell, but I wonder if it makes any sense to hold on to my stocks during a recession. Some investment managers are even recommending that people buy stock. Are they crazy or what?

A sharply declining stock market often presages a recession, and the 1990 stock performance appears to be no exception. The Dow Jones Industrial Average was down almost 10 percent through October 1990. But the large Dow stocks were stellar performers compared with smaller over-the-counter issues. The Over-the-Counter Composite Index was down 26 percent through the first ten months of 1990! Is there any reason to hold stocks in 1991? Isn't the economy going to get worse before it gets better? This chapter will help bring some sanity to the hysteria surrounding stock market investing, in which there are more opinions expressed than there are stocks to trade.

The 1990 bear market has increased investor anxiety

over stock investing, although most investors wisely have not abandoned stocks in the face of market uncertainty. On the other hand, many investors still overreact to unexpected events by making quick decisions to shift major portions of their investments. Others tend to ignore sudden changes in market conditions, which can be as detrimental as overreacting. Perhaps the most important attribute to have, in light of the uncertain stock market in 1991, is a sense of perspective. Stock investments have consistently outperformed interest-earning investments over the long term, usually by a wide margin. According to data compiled by Ibbotson Associates, the following average annual returns were earned by stocks, long-term government bonds, and Treasury bills in each of the last five decades.

	1940s	1950s	1960s	1970s	1980s
Stocks (S&P 500)	9.2%	19.4%	7.8%	5.9%	17.5%
Long-term government bonds	3.2	−0.1	1.4	5.5	12.6
Treasury bills	0.4	1.9	3.9	6.3	8.9

By looking at those statistics, you could conclude that you should have all your money in stocks. But that would be too risky—individual stocks do sometimes decline in value.

Even investors who choose to maintain a steady course in the face of market uncertainty are confused by the conflicting opinions of investment managers. Everyone has an opinion about the stock market, and no two experts agree. Some of the most respected names in the investment business, all successful money managers, provided the following opinions in one week in late 1990.

- Growth stocks have been beaten down so badly that soon their prices will skyrocket.
- The market will continue to plummet. Avoid stocks altogether well into 1991, at least.
- We are on the brink of a tremendous market rebound that will send the Dow Jones average to heretofore unheard-of heights.
- Small company stocks are irresistible at their present levels.
- The great bear market of the 1990s is upon us.

Do you see the danger in letting one person influence your investment decisions, or worse, letting one person make your investment decisions for you? Your best bet—listen to several experts, then make your own investment decisions, and invest with a long-term view. That way, you're not going to be overly influenced by current events and opinions.

Stock Investment Strategies for 1991

Successful stock investing requires patience and discipline, and 1991 will test these attributes sorely. There is nothing more painful for stockholders than a slow, agonizing drop in stock prices, with no end in sight. The temptation to cash out is overwhelming at times. The idea of buying stocks in such a market makes you wonder if you've lost your mind.

The following section summarizes some stock investment strategies for 1991 that are designed to keep you out of trouble and help you profit from the run-up in stock prices that inevitably follows a downturn. Remember, just as down stock markets precede recessions, stock prices usually begin to rebound during the latter stages of recessions. So, you don't want to avoid or pare down stock investments until economists tell us the recession is over, because if you wait until then, you will have missed part of the run up.

Form your own opinion about stock market conditions. The only way you can develop a disciplined and consistent strategy for dealing with market uncertainty in 1991 is to form your own opinion about where the stock market is going, not only in the next year but for years thereafter. That way, you decide what, if anything, to do with the stocks you already own and whether you want to add to your stock investments, or if you are new to the game, begin to make stock investments. If you are downright pessimistic about the future of our economy or fearful of what may eventually happen in the Mideast, you may want to avoid stocks altogether. At least, you wouldn't want to add to your investments until the crises are resolved. If you are not that worried, let me suggest an outlook that can help guide you through uncertain times. First, it is impossible to determine where stock prices will head in 1991. Of course, no one knows where stock prices are going to go in any given year— or in any given week, for that matter. No one should buy stocks with the expectation of holding them for only one year anyway. But what about the long run? If you are relatively confident about the long-term outlook of our economy, not only in 1991 and 1992, but in 1995 and at the turn of the century, you should be optimistic about stock prices in the long run. Hence, 1991 probably would not be such a bad year to make *some* stock investments, but don't make any major commitments or shifts in your investments. Stocks are reasonably priced at present, although they are certainly not cheap, at least by historical standards.

You have just read my opinion, which I formed by doing what anyone else can do—reading the financial pages of the newspaper, monitoring current stock market conditions, and rereading some good books on stock investing like Benjamin Graham's *Intelligent Investor*. Now do some research and write down your own opinion in the space provided below.

My opinion of stock market performance during 1991 is as follows: _____
_____
_____

My opinion of stock market performance over the rest of the decade is as follows: _____
_____
_____

Establish a plan for stock investing during the recession and stick to it. Once you have formed your own opinion about the direction of the stock market, you should plan what you're going to do. Admittedly, deciding to buy stocks when the market is flogged takes guts, but a consistent (and varied) approach is how to make money in investments. In other words, even if your plan is risky, stick to it—consistency pays.

Go global. There is a lot more to stock investing than buying U.S. stocks. In fact, U.S. stocks historically have performed rather poorly in comparison with foreign stocks. If you haven't already, commit some of your stock investment money, perhaps 10 to 20 percent, to foreign stocks. The only feasible way to play the foreign markets is to buy a good international mutual fund, such as those listed in Chapter Sixteen. Avoid single country funds or single region funds. Look for broad-based international funds that scour the world for the best investment opportunities.

Use dollar-cost averaging. Successful investors use a disciplined approach to buying stocks, which assures that they will build up a sizable portfolio over the years. Dollar-cost averaging (see Chapter Twelve) allows you to buy more shares in down markets, which, by the way, is one of the few benefits you could get from this recession.

Avoid unfamiliar investments. One unfortunate outcome of scary stock markets is that people sometimes make bad investments, which they wouldn't have made if they had their wits about them. If anything, this is a time to restrict your investments to stocks that are everyday names. Don't waste your hard-earned money on investment strategies that are unfamiliar to you, such as short selling, stock options, commodity futures, rare coins, art or collectibles. Don't stray from mainstream investments.

Don't become a gold bug. In past times of turbulence, many supposed experts have urged investors to load up on gold as a reliable hedge against economic and world turmoil. In the last year, gold has not behaved in that fashion. In fact, in response to world crisis and U.S. economic turbulence, gold prices have gone nowhere. Therefore, don't rely on gold to protect you through bad times.

Keep some of your powder dry. Sooner or later—probably later—stocks will be poised for a rebound. If you can afford it, keep some funds available to take advantage of stock investment opportunities that might present themselves in 1991 or later. The best temporary parking place for your money is cash-equivalent investments, described in Chapter Fourteen.

Reviewing Your Current Stock Investments

You need to review your stock and stock mutual fund investments to assure that they are consistent with current investment conditions and your outlook for 1991 and beyond. Unless you are an extraordinary stock and mutual fund picker, the performance of the stock portion of your portfolio in 1990 was disheartening. Don't be so disheartened that you would want to get out of stocks altogether, because stock investments should never be evaluated over such a short time period. Because of the delicate condition of the 1991 stock market, you will probably benefit by monitoring your stock investments a little more closely than you would under better market conditions.

With respect to individual stocks, consider weeding out any companies with poor prospects in this difficult economy. Plenty of publicly traded companies have poor prospects. Also, pay attention to industry trends, because even though you may own stock in a solid company, it could be battered if it's in an industry that is suffering. For example, many excellent regional and local banks have experienced big price declines because of guilt by association with the tremendous problems experienced by many money center banks.

Review your mutual funds periodically, as well. If you make the right mutual fund investment decisions to begin with, they should serve you well over many years. Nevertheless, some managers may have had difficulty in the turbulent markets of 1987 through 1990. One way to evaluate how your fund performed is to compare its total return performance against the average for its investment category. For example, if you own a growth and income fund, check its performance against the average performance for all growth-and-income funds. If your fund underperformed the average for its category for two consecutive years, you should probably sell it.

Most important, if the stock market continues to decline, don't become so discouraged over the performance of your stocks that you end up selling all or a major portion of them. That will probably be the worst time to sell. Remember what happened after the 500-point single-day drop in stock prices in October 1987. Frightened investors couldn't sell their stocks fast enough during the next week, and plenty of smart investors were more than happy to buy their shares. When confronted with market uncertainty, the best thing to do often is nothing.

Some Tips for Making Stock Investments in 1991

Nineteen ninety-one is not a year to speculate in no-name stocks. It is far better to select high-quality, financially strong companies, because no one is sure how bad this recession is going to get. If the recession deepens, and stock prices go down the drain, the highest-quality issues should suffer the least. Make sure stocks that you buy have many, or all, of the following characteristics.

Financial strength. Avoid companies that have a lot of debt, because they will have trouble during the recession.

Strong dividend-paying capacity. Companies with a consistent record of paying dividends, and the capacity to continue paying them even when business is down, will not only provide you with dividend income but also with a measure of security if the market keeps declining. Companies with a strong dividend-paying capacity tend not to decline as much as so-called growth companies, which typically pay little or no dividends.

Stable businesses. Look for companies that will thrive, or at least hold their own, during a recession, typically those involved in so-called recession-resistant businesses, such as grocery chains and pharmaceutical companies. A list of attractive industrial sectors appears in Chapter Sixteen.

Industry leaders. Select the best company in a given industry, because it has the best chance of performing reasonably well when the economy sours.

Low price-earnings ratio. Many investment experts suggest avoiding companies that sell at a high price in relation to their earnings (P/E). Look for good companies that trade at or below the average P/E ratio. This is doubly true when the stock market outlook is as uncertain as it is for 1991. If the market does turn down, high P/E ratio stocks tend to drop further in price than lower P/E ratio stocks.

Do your homework. This is hardly the time to rely on other people to tell you what to do with your money. Spend some time learning about investing and investments. Your local library probably has the two "bibles" that experienced investors rely on to help them make wise investment decisions. For stock investments, find the *Value Line Investment Survey,* and for mutual funds, look for the *Wiesenberger Investment Companies Service.* Learn to use the many resources that are available to help you become a better investor.

Buy Stock Mutual Funds to Obtain Diversification and Professional Management

Although many investors tend to run from their mutual funds during bad markets, they are, in fact, a preferable place for your stock investment money. Why? First, you get instant diversification with a stock mutual fund, and diversification is crucial in any market. Second, you get inexpensive professional management. You pay someone a very nominal sum— about one percent per year—to worry about your investments. There are many excellent stock mutual funds, including those listed in Chapter Sixteen. Incidentally, if you want to speculate in 1991 with a small portion of your money, consider investing in mutual funds that specialize in small, over-the-counter stocks. Small stocks were beaten down badly in 1990, and when the market returns, they could increase dramatically in price. But that's all speculation, and if the market really sours, small stocks will be beaten up again.

MAKE THE MOST OF YOUR STOCK INVESTMENTS DURING TOUGH TIMES

- ☐ Form your own opinion about current and future stock market conditions, so you can approach 1991 with a disciplined and consistent stock-investment strategy.
- ☐ Establish an investment plan for the recession, and stick to it.
- ☐ Consider investing in foreign-stock mutual funds.
- ☐ Use dollar-cost averaging to build up your stock portfolio.
- ☐ Make investments that you understand. Avoid unusual or complicated securities.
- ☐ Don't rely on gold as a safe haven amidst market turbulence.
- ☐ Keep some cash in reserve, to take advantage of a rebounding stock market.
- ☐ Review your current stock market investments, and eliminate any holdings with poor prospects in a difficult economy.
- ☐ Review your mutual fund investments, and eliminate those that consistently underperform their category averages.
- ☐ Any stock investments you make in 1991 should emphasize financially strong, dividend-paying companies that will hold up during a recession.
- ☐ Consider buying stock mutual funds to take advantage of their diversification and professional management.

MAKING THE RIGHT INTEREST-EARNING INVESTMENTS DURING TOUGH TIMES

I've got most of my savings invested at the local bank, in a money market deposit account and some CDs. From what I've been reading, the banks in this area are in real trouble. A couple have actually gone into bankruptcy. I'm worried about whether my money is safe, and some of my friends say there are much better places than the bank to put my money anyway.

CDs, money market funds, Treasury bills, corporate bonds, municipal bonds, Ginnie Maes, savings bonds—when it comes to making interest-earning investments, it is easy to get confused. The one thing they have in common is that they all pay interest. Beyond that, there can be significant differences, which I will explain. There are so many choices that finding the right investment is difficult, even in prosperous times. When the future of the economy is uncertain, it is hard even for the experts to get a handle on the direction of interest rates, and finding the right interest-earning investment becomes even more difficult. On the surface, interest-earning investing is pretty straightforward, with two basic objectives: to earn interest; and to get your original investment back when you sell it.

The current economic downturn adds considerable complexity to the evaluation of investments you own, as well as new investments. For example, no one knows whether interest rates will drop or rise as the recession progresses. Many factors could influence interest rates, including oil prices, the depth of the recession, and federal monetary policy. You also have to consider the safety of your investments, especially in the current economic environment. Holders of junk bonds and junk-bond mutual funds already understand that high yield means high risk, because they have suffered losses in their investments. Junk bonds are issued by corporations that already have a lot of debt or are in a shaky financial condition. Thus they have to pay a very high interest rate to entice people to lend them money. Now some experts are worried that even some higher quality bond issuers, including corporations and municipalities, may default on their debt obligations.

A Smorgasbord of Choice

No matter what your financial circumstances, interest rate outlook, or attitude toward risk, there are appropriate interest-earning investments for you. Interest-earning investments can be broken down into two categories. The first is cash-equivalent investments—interest-earning securities that can be readily converted into cash, with little or no change in principal value. In other words, you get your principal (your original investment) back—no more and no less—when you sell, plus you receive interest along the way. Cash-equivalent investments include money market accounts (sold by banks) and money market funds (sold by mutual funds), Treasury bills, and savings accounts. The interest paid on cash-equivalent investments fluctuates.

The second category of interest-earning securities is fixed-income investments. "Fixed income" means that the interest *rate* on the investment remains the same, or is fixed, regardless of what happens. However, the value of your principal will change with prevailing interest rates. Fixed-income investments have a maturity date, which is the date you get your original investment back. Some of the many available fixed-income investments are Treasury notes and bonds, mortgage-backed securities, such as Ginnie Maes; municipal bonds, and corporate bonds.

You can buy cash-equivalent or fixed-income investments directly, by buying individual securities through banks or stockbrokers, or indirectly, through a mutual fund where, in essence, you buy a portion of a diversified portfolio of interest-earning securities.

Although there is *never* any certainty about where interest rates are headed, it is particularly important to understand that fixed-income investments are subject to interest rate risk, especially in these times of potentially volatile interest rates. If you invest in a fixed-income security or mutual fund, and prevailing interest rates subsequently rise, the principal value of your investment will decline. It also works the other way. If interest rates decline after you have made your fixed-income investment, its value will increase. Unfortunately, many investors don't find out about interest-rate risk until after they have suffered a decline in the value of their investment. It is important to understand that the longer the maturity of a fixed-income security, the more its principal value will fluctuate as interest rates rise or fall.

Interest-earning Investment Strategies for 1991

Buy quality. Although there is no agreement on the outlook for interest rates, the experts do agree that in the current economic climate, you should buy only high-quality interest-earning investments, such as Treasury securities, certificates of deposit from federally insured banks, and high-grade corporate and municipal bonds. If you invest in interest-earning mutual funds, opt for funds that emphasize high-quality securities.

Diversify. The worse the economy gets, the more important it is to diversify. Unless you have only a very small amount of money to invest, don't concentrate your interest-earning investments in a single or very few securities. Select several different issues and, ideally, several different types of investment.

Ladder maturities. One of the best ways to hedge your bets in an uncertain interest-rate environment is to ladder (or stagger) your maturities—in other words, purchase equal amounts of bonds or certificates of deposit with maturities of, say, one, two, three, four, and five years. That way, if interest rates rise, you'll have a note or certificate coming due to reinvest at higher rates. You don't have to place a heavy bet on a single maturity.

Keep maturities relatively short. Even though longer-maturity interest-earning investments usually have slightly higher yields than shorter-maturity investments, there is not enough of a difference to justify the greater risks in longer-term investing. Too much uncertainty surrounds oil prices and inflation, at least until the Persian Gulf crisis is resolved. Therefore, most experts suggest keeping investment maturities rather short, generally well under ten years. On the other hand, if the yield on the bellwether thirty-year Treasury bond goes over 9 percent, you may want to reevaluate your investment strategy and lengthen the maturities on some of your interest-earning investments, to take advantage of a rate that is widely believed to be high and unsustainable over the long run. If you bet right, and interest rates subsequently decline, you have the best of both worlds: You are earning interest at a higher-than-prevailing rate, and you have a security that has increased in value because interest rates have declined. See Chapter Twelve for a further explanation of using the thirty-year Treasury bond yield as a bellwether to monitor interest-rate conditions.

Seek safe harbors if you expect the worst. If you're frightened about the prospects for the economy, stick with short-term, riskless securities. The best way to protect against market calamities is to put your money into riskless cash-equivalent investments, such as Treasury bills, government money market funds, and certificates of deposit from federally insured banks. Your interest income may not be as high as it could be, but that's a small price to pay if you otherwise would be losing sleep. Remember, however, that keeping your money in safe short-term securities could backfire, because recessions often end with dramatic stock-market rebounds that begin when the experts say stocks can only go down.

Extend maturities if you expect interest rates to drop. While I don't recommend that you try to speculate on interest rates, if you feel, as many do, that lower interest rates will be in the cards in late 1991 or 1992, you might want to extend the maturities on a *portion* of your interest-earning investments. As with all of your investments, however, don't place a heavy bet on any single issue or any single maturity. It is better to have a well-diversified array of investments, so you won't subject your hard-earned money to undue risk.

Shop around for yields. Yields on interest-earning

securities, even with otherwise identical features, vary. For example, chances are that interest paid on CDs varies among the banks in your community. Shopping around and comparing yields on CDs and other interest-earning securities can pay off handsomely. Don't confuse comparing yields with chasing yields—yield chasers want the highest possible yield and fail to recognize that high yield means high risk. Yield chasers favor junk bonds and junk-bond funds, which are a perfect investment—if you want high income and deteriorating principal!

Reviewing Your Current Interest-earning Investments

Because of the investment risks associated with the events in our economy, you need to review your current interest-earning holdings more carefully than you would under normal economic conditions. This is to assure that the financial stability of the company or municipality that issued the securities has not deteriorated since you bought them. Moreover, you need to be sure that your bank deposits are federally insured, in view of the problems in the banking industry. This would have been much less of a concern a few years ago. Also, check that you have appropriate diversification in your interest-earning investments.

Some Tips for Making Interest-earning Investments in 1991

As I mentioned earlier, you must pay particular attention to *quality* when buying interest-earning investments now. Avoid any temptation to invest in an individual security or mutual fund simply because it promises a high yield. The following comments may help you select appropriate investments in 1991.

- Since diversification is so important in scary markets, interest-earning mutual fund investments, always a sensible investment, make more sense than ever. Check to make sure that the fund invests a majority of the portfolio in high-quality securities. The easiest way to do that is to invest in a government bond fund or government money market fund. Intermediate-term bond funds make more sense than long-term bond funds in the current volatile interest-rate environment; you won't be subject to as much price volatility in the event of a significant shift in interest rates. Another way to protect your investments is to invest in more than one interest-earning mutual fund, each with a different investment objective.

- If you are making investments in a retirement-oriented account, like an IRA or Keogh plan, consider zero-coupon Treasuries. Zero-coupon Treasury securities pay no current interest. Instead, they are sold at a deep discount from face value, which is what you receive when they mature. A big advantage of "zeros" is that you don't have to worry about reinvesting the interest all the time, since they don't pay interest. These government-backed securities are excellent for retirement accounts, particularly when the yield on the long-term Treasury bond is 9 percent or higher.

- Also consider high-quality municipal bonds, because their after-tax return is probably better than what you'd receive from a taxable interest-earning security. Since many states and municipalities are currently having fiscal problems, select only bonds that are highly rated by the bond rating services—typically "general obligation" bonds— in other words bonds that are backed by the full faith, credit, and taxing powers of the issuing municipality. Insured municipal bonds—interest and principal payments are guaranteed by an independent company—add an additional level of comfort, although many experts predict that if an economic situation occurred where there were massive defaults on municipal obligations—although this is very unlikely—municipal bond insurers might not be able to make good on all their obligations.

How Safe Is Your Bank?

Many people are concerned about the safety of their banks, savings and loan institutions, and credit unions. Hardly a day goes by without some bad news on the banking front. Numerous deposit institutions have been liquidated or merged with stronger ones in the last few years. Many financial institutions either have filed for bankruptcy or are on the verge of bankruptcy. In a few instances, depositors actually lost money. For the most part, however, customers need not fear for the safety of their deposits as long as the banks are federally insured. Most commercial and mutual savings banks are insured by the Federal Deposit Insurance Corporation (FDIC). Most savings and loans and savings banks are insured by the Federal Savings and Loan Insurance Corporation (FSLIC). The National Credit Union Association (NCUA) insures the vast majority of credit unions. The federal government backs the insurance offered by these organizations, should their reserves prove insufficient.

If your deposits are placed with federally insured institutions, you need not be concerned, as long as your deposits stay within certain limits. For the most part, deposits up to $100,000 are fully insured, which is all most of us need. If you are fortunate enough to have more than $100,000 on deposit, you need to check with the institution to make sure that your money is fully insured. There are ways to structure deposits so that you can insure more than $100,000— for example, through joint accounts. Alternatively, you could spread your deposits among more than one account. The $100,000 limit is per institution, per account, and per investor.

What happens if your bank, savings and loan, or credit union fails? The regulators step in to liquidate assets, and insured depositors can expect to be paid shortly after the closing. There have been delays in some instances, but insured depositors got their money back.

If you have deposits at an institution that is *not* federally insured, you should be concerned. While these banks may have private or state insurance funds, history has shown that such insurance cannot always make good on depositors' claims. It is best to stick with federally insured institutions.

One final note: The recent savings and loan debacle has caused Congress to look at placing further limitations on federal deposit insurance. Congress may enact laws at any time that reduce or restrict, but don't eliminate, federal deposit insurance. If such legislation is enacted, find out how it will affect your bank, savings and loan, or credit union deposits.

MAKING THE MOST OF YOUR INTEREST-EARNING INVESTMENTS DURING TOUGH TIMES

☐ Try not to limit your interest-earning investments to a single type of security, like CDs. There are probably many different categories of interest-earning investments that are appropriate for you.

☐ Understand the interest-rate risk inherent in owning interest-earning securities and mutual funds.

☐ Stick to high-quality interest-earning investments.

☐ Diversify your interest-earning investment portfolio.

☐ Hedge your bets by laddering the maturities on your interest-earning investments.

☐ Until interest rates rise and/or the economy settles down, keep to interest-earning securities with short maturities.

☐ Shop around for the most attractive yields.

☐ If you are particularly worried about how the economy will affect your investments, consider placing your money in cash-equivalent investments.

☐ Review your investments to make sure you are not taking undue risk in the current economic climate.

☐ Don't overlook the many advantages of investing in interest-earning mutual funds.

☐ Consider buying zero-coupon Treasuries for tax-deferred retirement accounts.

☐ Consider high-quality municipal bonds if your after-tax return is higher than from equivalent taxable securities.

☐ Make sure your banks, savings and loans, and credit unions are federally insured.

☐ If you have over $100,000 in a single financial institution, organize the accounts so that all of the money is federally insured.

☐ If Congress limits the amount of federal deposit insurance that is available to each depositor, review the status of your accounts.

15

MAKING THE RIGHT
REAL ESTATE INVESTMENTS
DURING TOUGH TIMES

This real estate market looks too luscious to pass up. The auction notices in the Sunday paper fill up two pages, and I heard the Resolution Trust Corporation, which picked up all of those bum S&L properties, is almost giving them away. It looks like the perfect time to buy a couple of properties for a song.

Real estate has traditionally been one of the best ways for people of average means to get rich. But, as many real estate investors have found out and will continue to find out in 1991, it is also possible to lose a lot of money. If you own real estate, you may be troubled by the deterioration of the real estate market or delighted that prices have held firm, depending largely on where you own property. If you are a potential real estate buyer, you are undoubtedly tempted by the apparent bargains flooding the market. This chapter will provide some guidance for people who own, or are interested in purchasing, investment real estate in a perilous market. Home ownership will not be discussed in this chapter. Advice for homeowners appears in Chapter Twenty-two, and opportunities for first-time homeowners are reviewed in Chapter Twenty-four.

The Three Ways to Invest in Real Estate

Real estate investing can play an important role in a well-balanced investment portfolio. Real estate is considered the third major investment category, after stock and interest-earning investments. Many people choose not to invest in real estate, and this is perfectly okay. If you are interested in real estate investing, there are three ways to participate.

1. **Own-it-yourself.** Of the three ways to own real estate, purchasing it yourself provides the greatest returns—and the greatest risks. There are two types of own-it-yourself real estate. *Income-producing real estate* can range from a rented condominium unit to an apartment building, to commercial property. If you purchase wisely—in other words, don't overpay for the property—you can enjoy good cash flow, possible tax benefits, and significant long-term appreciation in value. Many people, however, lack the time or the inclination to manage income-producing real estate. *Undeveloped land* ties up a lot of money for a long time. Land in particularly desirable areas is very expensive, but with some luck, will appreciate considerably in value.

2. **Real estate limited partnerships.** Real estate limited partnerships are a way for people to invest in specific properties at a relatively low cost—generally $5,000 or more—and not have to manage the properties. Real estate limited partnerships were once a very common way to invest in real estate, but they have fallen on hard times. If you have invested in limited partnerships in the past, you are probably painfully aware of the shock waves going through this industry.

Overbuilding in many locales, tax reform, weak real estate markets, and in some instances, greedy general partners caused the downfall.

3. **Real estate investment trusts.** A real estate investment trust (REIT) is a corporation that invests in real estate or mortgages. REIT shares trade on the stock exchange, so for no more than the cost of buying some shares of stock, you can participate in the real estate market.

Real Estate Investment Strategies for 1991

In many areas of this country, the real estate industry is entering the recession in such a weakened condition that experienced investors are justifiably reluctant to make major real estate commitments. There still are opportunities for the venturesome, but given the potential continued downward pressure on real estate prices and the difficulty of obtaining bank financing, the real estate industry in 1991 will be dead in the water in many regions of the country. While the real estate investment professional may be able to identify and take advantage of attractive investments, the part-time real estate investor is ill-advised to play this market until conditions improve. If you plan to play this market, please consider the following:

- I advise investors who want to consider real estate investments in 1991 to purchase parcels that are close to home, since real estate is so closely tied to local economies. Those who are familiar with the real estate market in their local community enjoy a significant advantage over those who try to purchase real estate in an unfamiliar locale. But be forewarned. The bottom has not been reached in every market, and real estate conditions vary from region to region, and from one type of property to the next. In general, apartments seem to have the most potential in the early 1990s, due to the aging population and the growth of single-parent households.

- There are distressed properties in many regions of the country, and investors may be attracted to the appealing notion of obtaining a real estate parcel at a foreclosure auction or through the Resolution Trust Corporation (RTC), which is charged with disposing of the foreclosed properties of defunct savings and loans. Both methods of acquiring property are fraught with difficulty, however. Buying real estate at auction requires extensive research before bidding on the property, which will generally be sold "as is," without contingencies for inspection and without warranty. Foreclosed properties sold at auction are often in poor condition and there may be liens on the property or clouds in the title. Dealing with the RTC can be a time-consuming bureaucratic nightmare, although a local real estate broker may be able to assist you.

- Real estate limited partnerships will offer investors little in 1991. The industry is still paying for its excesses of the 1980s, and billions of dollars worth of real estate limited partnerships are now almost worthless. The industry is desperately trying to stay in business, which should concern potential limited partnership investors. Although the deals are structured much more sensibly than they were when they were packaged as tax shelters, most deals rely on price appreciation at a time when prices are moving downward.

- The outlook for real estate investment trusts in 1991 is also guarded. Many REITs have invested in major commercial properties, and a slowing economy is exacerbating an already competitive leasing environment. And the specter of the RTC's vast holdings of real estate flooding an already depressed market has cast a pall over the REIT industry and held down prices.

Review Your Current Real Estate Investments

If you own income-producing real estate. Chances are 1991 is *not* the time to consider selling your income-producing real estate, although some regions of the country will manage to enjoy relatively robust real estate markets. If the economy continues to deteriorate, you may be confronted with an unusually competitive market for tenants, and you must plan for the possibility that you may have to go to unusual lengths to retain or attract tenants. Also, build up your cash reserves in anticipation of potentially more difficult times. You want to try to avoid being forced to sell your property in this weak environment.

If you own real estate limited partnerships. If you are a limited partnership owner, you probably are not a happy camper. The secondary market for limited partnerships, such as it is, will only pay top dollar for successful partnership investments, which you wouldn't want to sell in the first place. In short, there isn't much you can do about a soured partnership.

If you own REITs. Unless you are unusually lucky or wise, your real estate investment trust holdings probably have performed much like other stocks you own. In a word, badly. The outlook for 1991 isn't very rosy either. Your decision as to whether to hold on may depend on the kind of income you are receiving from your REIT. Many have attractive dividend yields at present, although given the outlook for the real estate industry in general, these yields are hardly assured. The decision to hold or sell REITs should hinge on whether the REIT is likely to perform well or not over the next year.

Some Tips for Making Real Estate Investments in 1991

As the above discussion suggests, you will need considerable intestinal fortitude to make real estate investments in 1991. In spite of all the negatives, however, some investors will probably do quite well. A few professional investors have indicated that they have not seen a better opportunity for investing in real estate in years. Still, this is the kind of opportunity that only experienced real estate investors can exploit. What troubles me is a new investor thinking that he or she can take advantage of this market weakness and buy properties for a pittance.

- If you have been investing and managing income-producing real estate, you may be able to take advantage of opportunities in your locale. Otherwise, steer clear of these risky investments.
- Real estate limited partnerships will be too risky to bet your money on in 1991. One deal in a hundred will be worthwhile. Best advice: avoid making any new partnership investments until the real estate market turns around. Remember that the people who sell you these partnerships are always going to tell you that the market has turned around.
- If you want to play the real estate market, perhaps the REIT route is best. It certainly is cheapest. Real estate investments are renowned for their extreme boom/bust cycles, and it's at the perceived bottom of a cycle that experienced real estate professionals jump in and reap extraordinary returns. The REIT vehicle was legislated into existence specifically to enable the smaller investor to participate in such gains. Since REIT prices have been beaten down so badly, such an opportunity *might* present itself, but it would be a spec-

ulation. If you want to take the plunge, look for REITs that specialize in apartments or cater to the elderly. They should hold up relatively well during a recession.

MAKING THE MOST OF REAL ESTATE INVESTMENTS IN 1991

☐ If you are new to real estate investing, learn about the opportunities associated with each of the three ways to invest in real estate.

☐ Unless you already own real estate, don't purchase any properties in distressed markets. True bargains are hard to come by.

☐ Be wary of real estate limited partnerships. The industry is in disarray, and the deals offered are far from sure winners.

☐ If you own income-producing real estate, carefully evaluate local market conditions, and prepare for any problems you foresee.

☐ Carefully selected REITs offer a low-cost way to speculate in the real estate industry.

16

NINETY-ONE GOOD STOCKS AND MUTUAL FUNDS FOR 1991

Like most people, I don't have a lot of confidence in the stock and bond markets, but I don't want to move my investments into money markets because I might miss a rebound in stock prices. Maybe I'm just a dreamer, but I'd like to be able to invest my money in some stocks and bonds that I wouldn't have to worry about during this recession.

It isn't easy investing when the markets are particularly skittish. During these times it makes a lot of sense to stay with investments you know well: stocks of companies that are leaders in industries, which shouldn't fare too poorly during a recession, and mutual funds that have proven records of strong performance in both good and bad markets. The following lists of recession-resistant industry sectors, top stocks to own now, stocks with excellent dividend payment records, and mutual fund leaders can help you make wise investments in a tricky market.

Defensive Stock Groups

You've probably heard a lot of talk lately about defensive investing. This does not mean investing in weapons manufacturers. A defensive investment is made primarily to protect yourself against a decline in stock prices. The following is a list of defensive stock groups, which should, but won't necessarily, perform better than other groups in a recession. Note that stocks in these groups produce goods or services that we use under any economic conditions. They are often called recession-resistant stocks, although there is no telling how resistant they will be to the recession of 1991.

Defensive Stock Groups

Beverages
Cosmetics
Drugs
Foods
Health Care
Liquor
Supermarkets
Telephones
Tobacco
Utilities

The Top Twenty-five Stocks to Own Now

The following is a list of twenty-five excellent stocks to own amidst all the stock market uncertainty. This is a time to invest in quality companies, and this list contains many of the best companies in the U.S. Most of these firms are in defensive stock groups, and they are expected to hold up very well during the recession. To find out more about these companies, check the *Value Line Investment Survey* at your local library.

Top Twenty-five Stocks	Line of Business
Abbott Labs	Diversified health-care products
Anheuser-Busch	Largest U.S. brewer; baking

Bausch & Lomb	Vision care and instruments
Borden	Dairy and food products, chemicals
British Telecom	Telecommunication services in the U.K.
CPC International	Grocery products, corn wet milling
Coca-Cola	Syrup and juice distributor; films
ConAgra	Bakery flour; feeds; poultry
Crown Cork & Seal	Metal cans; closures
Eli Lilly	Ethical drugs; agricultural chemicals
General Mills	Consumer foods; restaurants
IBM	Largest business-machine manufacturer
Johnson & Johnson	Health-care products
MAPCO	Coal; LP-gas pipeline; crude oil
Merck	Ethical drugs; specialty chemicals
Bristol-Myers Squibb	Pharmaceuticals; medical products; nonprescription health products; toiletries
PepsiCo	Soft drinks; snack foods; food service
Philip Morris	Cigarettes; brewing; soft drinks
Procter & Gamble	Household; personal care; food products
Ralston Purina	Pet foods; bakery products; batteries
Schering-Plough	Pharmaceuticals; consumer products
Schlumberger	Oil-field services; electronics
Sherwin Williams	Paint and varnish manufacturer

Unilever	Consumer goods
Wal-Mart Stores	Discount stores

Companies with Strong Dividend-Payment Records

One approach to buying stocks when you fear that the market may continue to deteriorate is to pick companies that have a consistent history of paying generous dividends. In a bear market, these companies tend to decline less in price than companies that pay no dividend at all or pay dividends erratically, since investors are confident that the dividends will keep coming through thick and thin. The following is a list of dividend-paying all-stars. Each company has a record of increasing its dividend in each of the last five years, and many have increased dividends for fifteen years or more. They all have strong balance sheets with little debt, and the minimum annual dividend payment rate was 3 percent of market value. Check on the current financial position of these companies before investing, by obtaining reports from stockbrokerage firms or by referring to the *Value Line Investment Survey,* because the strength of a company can deteriorate rapidly in the kind of recession we're going through.

Company	Line of Business
American Business Products	Business supplies
American National Insurance	Insurance
Aon Corporation	Insurance
Banc One Corporation	Commercial banking
H&R Block	Tax preparation

Borden, Inc.	Dairy and food products; chemicals
Clorox Co.	Household products; special foods
Consolidated Papers	Enamel printing paper
Deluxe Corp.	Check printing
Diebold	ATM machines
Emerson Electric	Electric parts
Fifth Third Bancorp	Commercial banking
First Wachovia Corp.	Commercial banking
Gannett Co.	Newspapers, TV/radio
General Mills	Consumer foods; restaurants
General Motors	Largest automotive products manufacturer
Genuine Parts	Auto replacement parts distributor
Hanson PLC	Industrial holding company in the U.K. & U.S.
John C. Harland Co.	Check printing
Hartford Steam Boiler & Insurance	Insurance
Hubbell Inc.	Electrical parts
Jefferson-Pilot Corp.	Insurance
K mart Corp.	Discount department stores
Kimberly-Clark	Consumer paper products; newsprint
Marsh & McLennan	Insurance brokerage and agency service
Minnesota Mining & Manufacturing (3M)	Tapes, adhesives
NBD Bancorp	Savings & commercial banking

National City Corp.	Commercial banking
National Gas & Oil	Natural gas supplies
National Presto Industries	Small appliances; defense products
National Service Industries	Lighting equipment
J.C. Penney	Discount department stores
Pfizer	Drugs
Philip Morris	Cigarettes; brewing; soft drinks
Royal Trustco Ltd.	Canadian trust company
Thomas & Betts	Electrical parts
UST Inc.	Snuff, tobacco; wines; pipes
Unilever N.V.	Consumer goods
Wells Fargo & Co.	Commercial banking
Westinghouse Electric	Manufacturer of electrical/ nuclear power equipment

Best Mutual Funds to Own Now

Mutual funds are investment companies that pool investors' money and manage it. Mutual funds are a great way to invest in any market, and the diversification and professional management they provide makes particularly good sense during uncertain markets. There are a lot of very good mutual funds. Some of them are listed below. All are no-load funds, which means you won't pay a sales commission to buy them. Information is just a phone call away, and the numbers are provided. The funds are classified according to the types of securities they invest in. Besides contacting the individual fund companies, you can find information on each of these funds, as well as explanations of the fund categories, in the *Wiesenberger Investment Companies Service*, which can be found in most libraries.

Maximum-capital-gains Funds (seek maximum capital appreciation by investing in stocks of higher growth potential and risk)
  Neuberger Berman Partners (800-877-9700)
  Scudder Capital Growth (800-225-2470)
  Twentieth Century Growth (800-345-2021)

Growth Funds (holdings are made up primarily of growth stocks)
  CGM Capital Development (800-345-4048)
  Janus Fund (800-525-3713)
  Twentieth Century Select (800-354-2021)

Growth and Income Funds (seek both current income and long-term capital appreciation)
  Dodge & Cox Stock Fund (415-981-1710)
  Fidelity Fund (617-523-1919)
  Vanguard Index Trust (800-662-7447)

Balanced Funds (invest in both bonds and stocks)
  CGM Mutual Fund (800-345-4048)
  Lindner Dividend Fund (314-727-5305)
  Wellington Fund (800-662-7447)

Gold Funds (invest in gold and other precious metals, either by owning shares of mining companies or by owning bullion)
  Lexington Goldfund (800-526-0057)
  Vanguard Specialized—Gold/Precious Metals (800-662-7447)

International Stock Funds (invest in stocks traded on exchanges outide the U.S.)
  Fidelity Overseas (800-544-6666)
  Price (T. Rowe) International Stock (800-638-5660)
  Scudder International (800-225-2470)

Flexible Funds (management, at its discretion, may invest in stocks, bonds, or both)
  Fidelity Puritan (800-544-6666)

Asset-allocation Fund (invest in a broadly diversified group of stocks, bonds, and other securities)
  USAA Cornerstone (800-531-8000)

Corporate Bond Funds (invest in bonds and notes of corporations)
  Dreyfus A Bonds Plus (800-554-4611)
  Fidelity Intermediate Bond (800-544-6666)
  Neuberger Berman Limited Maturity Bond (800-877-9700)

U.S. Government Securities Funds (invest in U.S. Treasury securities and/or other U.S. government agency securities)
  Vanguard Fixed Income–GNMA Fund (800-662-7447)
  Value Line U.S. Government Securities Fund (800-223-0818)

Municipal Bond Funds (invest in tax-exempt bonds issued by states, cities, and other local governments)
  SteinRoe Managed Municipals (800-338-2550)
  Vanguard Municipal Bond-Intermediate (800-662-7447)

TACKLING SPECIAL SITUATIONS

17

IF YOU LOSE YOUR JOB

I lost my job yesterday after eleven years at the company. I was tempted not to tell my family last night, but I did. I just don't know how we're going to make it financially.

Losing your job is traumatic under any circumstances, but particularly when unemployment is high and job prospects seem bleak. The current recession is unique in that vast numbers of management-level workers are going to find themselves unemployed. In previous recessions, blue-collar employees suffered the brunt of the layoffs. Unemployment levels have been rising and probably will continue to do so. If you've recently joined the ranks of the unemployed, you need to attend to two very important but difficult matters. First, you must strive to overcome the personal anxiety you almost certainly are experiencing. Second, you need to assess your financial situation, so you can cope with the loss of income. Above all, don't panic. You *can* and *will* overcome this temporary setback.

Overcoming Anxiety

Before you can get your feet back on the ground, you must overcome the inevitable psychological and

emotional stress. Most people go through three stages
of anxiety.

1. First, there is the *immediate panic* associated
with the loss of employment. Your first reaction may
be to hide this fact from your family and friends. Some
people even go to the extreme of leaving home every
day as if they were going to their job. Avoid this
temptation. Your family and friends will provide enormous support, and the more support you have, the
easier it will be for you to get back on your feet and
find another, probably better, job.

2. **Guilt and lack of self-worth.** After your initial
panic has subsided, you may begin to blame yourself
for your plight. You may feel that you have let yourself
and your family down, and are convinced that job
prospects are going to be pretty poor. Obviously,
these feelings are not going to help your situation, but
you need to recognize that you are likely to go through
this stage.

3. **Anger at the world.** Finally, you will begin to feel
angry about your situation, and it is not until you get
through this last stage that you will be in the frame of
mind to present yourself to a prospective employer
convincingly. This stage typically leads to renewed
self-confidence and determination.

Most importantly, you must be willing to ask for
help. Other people can offer emotional support and
can be a source of information about new employment
opportunities. The sooner you face up to your situation, the sooner you will be able to evaluate your
financial situation, and the sooner you will be able to
begin the search for a new job.

Coping with the Loss of Income

In spite of the emotional trauma, you must evaluate your current financial situation realistically, so you can adjust to your temporarily changed financial circumstances. This is particularly important, since you have lost your job during a recession, and therefore, you may spend more time unemployed than you would during more prosperous times. You need to address the following matters.

- Understanding severance benefits
- Assuring continuation of health and life insurance coverage
- Applying for unemployment compensation benefits
- Summarizing your ready resources
- Reducing spending
- Preparing a budget

Understanding severance benefits. Be sure you understand your employer's severance benefits, such as salary continuation, payment for accrued vacation, and insurance benefits. If you are about to be laid off or have just been laid off, it may be possible to negotiate additional severance benefits from your employer. Experts suggest that this be done within a day or two of the layoff, when the employer is most apt to respond to your appeal.

Assuring continuation of health and life insurance coverage. It is advantageous to continue to carry your employer-provided health and life insurance coverage, as well as all other insurance coverage. Most employers are required by law to allow you to continue your company health insurance plan for up to eighteen months without a medical checkup, as long as you pay the premiums. While the premiums may be steep, you should not go one minute without health insurance coverage. Alternatively, you might be able to save some money by purchasing a temporary insurance policy, which usually covers periods from three months to one year. Acquiring a new policy, even a temporary one, may require a medical checkup and/or preclude preexisting conditions. Be sure that the temporary health insurance coverage does not leave any gaps that could cost you dearly when you can least afford it.

If your employer does not continue your life insurance coverage, you may be able to convert your employer's group policy to an individual policy. Otherwise, you may be able to purchase low-cost life insurance coverage to replace your company-provided policy by shopping around for the best rates. See Chapter Ten for tips on acquiring and maintaining adequate insurance coverage when times are tough.

Applying for unemployment compensation benefits. If you've been let go, you are entitled to collect unemployment compensation benefits. Strange as it may seem, some people, perhaps out of sense of pride or embarrassment, don't want to collect these benefits, even though they are eligible. By all means apply for unemployment compensation as soon as you lose your job.

Summarizing your ready resources. Most everyone is suffering from the current economic downturn, and if you are recently unemployed, you are doubly affected. Your primary financial concern is how you're going to meet your financial obligations during your unemployment period, so you should begin by summarizing your ready resources—cash that is now available, as well as any investments that can be sold and converted into cash in a short period of time. The following table will help you summarize your ready resources. Once you know how much or how little you have available, you can begin to prepare a budget that will sustain you during a period of unemployment.

Reducing spending. Unless you are one of the few who are blessed with abundant ready resources, you are probably going to have to reduce your spending for a while, at least. Before you can do this, you should summarize your past spending patterns so that you can identify ways to cut expenses. Chapters Five and Six will assist you in this process.

SUMMARY OF READY RESOURCES

Cash in bank accounts	$_____
Savings, money market accounts	_____
CDs and other interest-earning investments	_____
Stock investments	_____
Mutual funds	_____
Other resources available	_____
Total ready resources	$_____

Preparing a budget. Once you have figured out what income and resources you have ready and how you have been spending your money, you are ready to prepare a budget, which ideally should insure that you will be able to meet important bills over the next six months. The budget work sheet provided in Chapter Five may be used for this purpose. First, you should project your income, including any severance benefits, unemployment benefits, income from your spouse's job, and investment income, unless you will have to liquidate those investments to meet living expenses. Next, summarize your expected expenses, starting with the expenses that must be paid—rent/mortgage and groceries, for example—and ending with those expenses that can be forgone—dining out and vacations. After you have summarized your projected expenses, you can compare them with your expected income and decide how you are going to close the gap between income (probably too little) and expenses (probably too much). The key to dealing with the financial strain of unemployment is to reduce expenses as much as possible, and if your unemployment income is insufficient to meet your reduced expense level, you will have to use ready resources to help meet expenses.

A few other tips:

☐ Keep up with your mortgage payments, since your house is probably your largest investment. See Chapter Twenty-two, which includes comments on what to do if you fall behind on your mortgage payments.

☐ You may be able to borrow from your company salary reduction plan (401(k)) or pension plan. But tapping into these important retirement plans should not be taken lightly.

☐ Other retirement accounts, such as IRAs and deferred annuities, can also be tapped, although you'll incur a penalty.

☐ Consider part-time work to augment your income. You'll be surprised at how much part-time work is available during a recession.

☐ Resist the temptation that many laid-off people have of starting their own business. A recession is almost never the time to do this.

☐ If it appears likely that you are going to have trouble meeting your obligations to creditors, be sure to contact them and work out a more comfortable payment schedule. See Chapter Twenty-one for more information on dealing with creditors when times are tough.

Your Job Search

Whether your financial situation is pretty good or pretty dismal, you need to approach the job search with the same enthusiasm and dedication that you would apply to any new and challenging task. The fact that everything you read about the plight of the unemployed during the recession is downright depressing doesn't mean that your prospects are bleak. Sure, you'll be discouraged by any rejections, but you *will* succeed sooner rather than later as long as you sustain your effort.

While you are unemployed, consider doing volunteer work. It will keep you busy during time not spent looking for work. Also, it can account for the period of unemployment on your résumé, and employers may be impressed by your resourcefulness during a time when far too many unemployed people sit at home feeling sorry for themselves.

IF YOU LOSE YOUR JOB

- [ ] Above all, don't panic. You will survive this setback, just as you have survived and will survive the other setbacks we all experience during our lifetimes.
- [ ] Accept the fact that you are going to experience a lot of stress, particularly right after you lose your job. Seek and welcome the support of your family and friends.
- [ ] Take advantage of unemployment compensation benefits that you are entitled to.
- [ ] Continue or replace all important employer-provided insurance coverage.
- [ ] Summarize the resources you have available to meet living expenses during the period of unemployment.

☐ Budget carefully for the future by analyzing past spending patterns, determining ways you can cut back on expenses, and figuring out where you are going to obtain sufficient resources.

☐ Begin your job search quickly and enthusiastically.

☐ Keep yourself occupied. Consider doing volunteer work.

18

IF YOU THINK YOU MIGHT LOSE YOUR JOB

My company is having a terrible time with the recession. They haven't laid anybody off yet, but rumors are circulating that they may soon. My area may be vulnerable to a layoff if one does come, and I don't have much seniority. Things are hard enough right now with the way the economy is going, but I don't even want to think about what would happen if I lose my job.

If you are one of the many people who fear that they may lose their job because of the current recession or for some other reason, you should start planning now. Even if you don't lose your job, you won't be any worse off for making these preparations. Preparing in advance for the loss of a job can reduce the disruptions to your career and personal finances that are almost inevitable if you become unemployed.

Evaluating Your Job Status

Assess the situation. Perhaps the first thing to do if you are worried about losing your job is to assess, as realistically as possible, the probability that this might happen. Rumors of massive layoffs can circulate around some large companies for years without any occurring. Many more people fret about being laid off than actually join the ranks of the unemployed. While these economic times make it more difficult to speculate on company layoffs, you still should try to make an objective assessment of the likelihood that you are going to lose your job and when it might occur. Has the company gone through previous layoffs? How essential is your department, and how is it doing during the recession?

Examine job opportunities. Should you look for another job? If your assessment leads you to believe that you may be one of the victims, you may not want to wait for the axe to fall. Since current economic conditions make job hunting even more difficult than it is normally, you may benefit by beginning your job search now, but do it discreetly, of course.

Arm yourself with information. Another advantage of being realistic about your job prospects is that you can prepare for the fateful day, not only from a financial standpoint, which is discussed below, but also from the standpoint of dealing with your employer. Even though most layoff victims anticipate that they are going to lose their jobs, they are often so shocked when the time comes that they are not in a position to negotiate a better severance arrangement. Your employer is much more likely to accommodate your needs if you express them immediately at the time of severance. Experts suggest you will be able to do this much better if you are prepared for the layoff. Remember, the company is as uncomfortable about letting people go as the employees are about being let go. Even if you are not in a position to improve your severance arrangement, by being mentally prepared you will be well on your way to landing on your feet and finding another job.

Review Your Financial Status

You can take several financial actions prior to your expected unemployment that can help reduce your fiscal duress. Incidentally, many of these suggestions are a good idea under any circumstances, not just under threat of imminent unemployment.

Prepare a survival budget. You should prepare a budget that assumes that you will be unemployed for a period of six months. First, estimate your income during unemployment, including unemployment compensation benefits and severance payments. Look carefully at your past expenses, and classify them according to expenses that must be paid (such as the mortgage or rent), necessities that could be reduced somewhat in the event of dire financial straits, and discretionary expenses like clothing, vacations, and meals at restaurants. Chapter Five provides guidance on preparing family budgets. If your expected income during unemployment is going to be insufficient to meet your expenses, and it probably will, you can plan how to close the gap. This will probably involve a combination of reducing your living expenses and finding other sources of income. See Chapter Seventeen for information on actual job loss.

Reduce current spending in order to increase savings. The two best things that you can do to prepare for financial adversity go hand in hand: reduce your current level of spending and increase your savings. Setting aside some savings now may come in very handy in helping you meet your living expenses later if you become unemployed. A financial cushion is the best way to soften the trauma of unemployment. It is bad enough that you may have to go through the job-hunting process. But it would be doubly unfortunate to have to worry about making ends meet. So take action now to increase or begin a savings program. Chapter Six provides ideas for reducing your expenses, and Part III offers guidance on investing your savings wisely.

Manage your debt. If you have outstanding debts, such as auto and credit card loans, you may be wondering whether you should reduce them in anticipation of unemployment rather than increase your savings level. In general, if you are concerned about losing your job, you should be careful not to fall behind in debt payments, but you're better off putting extra money in savings rather than further reducing your debt. Why? If you do lose your job, you may have to dip into savings to meet living expenses. If you had used the money to reduce your debts, this potential financial cushion would not be available to you. Paying down high-interest debt is a good idea under more normal economic circumstances. Your financial uncertainty, however, requires that you establish a generous emergency fund rather than reduce your indebtedness.

Adjust your tax withholding. If you are quite certain that you are going to be laid off, you might want to arrange to have less income tax withheld from your paycheck (by increasing the number of exemptions) so that your take-home pay is increased. This will provide extra income to use when you are unemployed. Since your income will almost certainly drop when you are laid off, the taxes owed will probably balance out by the end of the year, even though you decreased your tax withholdings while you were still employed.

Defer large expenditures. Now is *not* the time to make any large purchases, such as a new car or home improvements. These commitments should be deferred at least until you are confident that your job is not in jeopardy. Even then, you should be very careful about making major financial commitments when the economy is on the rocks. Many people are tempted to make large expenditures during economic downturns because sellers of these products and services—automobile dealers and home improvement contractors, for example—offer bargain prices to attract customers when business is slow. People who are blessed with abundant cash reserves and certain future income prospects may take advantage of these offers, but you would be better off deferring all major purchases until your job uncertainty is resolved. Besides, the bargain prices aren't that much lower, believe me.

Plan for continuity of insurance coverage. One of the worst things people can do during a period of financial adversity is to let their insurance coverage lapse. Stories abound of people who thought they couldn't afford to continue their health-insurance coverage, only to find their finances wiped out by an uninsured illness. Be sure to include a provision in your budget for paying insurance premiums. Also, decide ahead of time how you are going to replace your employer-provided health and life insurance when it expires. Your company is probably required to allow you to continue your group health coverage for a period of eighteen months after termination so long as you pay the premiums. Look into it.

Review your investments. If you are expecting to lose your job, you should review your investments, for two reasons. First, you need to assess how much of your invested funds can be readily converted into cash to meet living expenses if the need arises. Second, you may decide to sell some of your low-yield investments, which pay little or no dividends, such as many stocks. You can reinvest this money into interest-earning securities that will provide you with higher current income to help meet expenses when your salary is temporarily eliminated. You have to weigh the tax effects of any investment transactions, however. For example, it may not make sense to sell very-low-tax-basis stock investments in order to buy interest-earning investments, since the capital gains taxes you will have to pay after the sale will reduce the resources available for reinvestment in interest-earning securities. See other chapters of this book for recommendations on investing in uncertain times.

IF YOU THINK YOU'RE GOING TO LOSE YOUR JOB:

- ☐ Make a realistic assessment of the possibility that you might lose your job and when you might lose it.
- ☐ Prepare yourself mentally for a potential job loss so that it will not be devastating if and when it happens.
- ☐ Prepare a budget that assumes you will be laid off and includes a plan of action that balances income and expenses.
- ☐ Increase your savings rate or begin to save, so you will have a cushion if you lose your job.
- ☐ Don't make any large expenditures while your job outlook is uncertain.
- ☐ Plan now to assure that you maintain adequate insurance coverage during your period of unemployment.
- ☐ Make sure your savings are invested appropriately in light of your uncertain financial future.

EVALUATING EARLY-RETIREMENT INCENTIVE PLANS

My company has offered an early-retirement incentive plan to everyone in my department. I wasn't planning to retire for a few more years, but their offer seems so attractive. I like my job, but I might get laid off anyway if things get worse. I don't know what to do.

Early-retirement incentive programs, also called window incentives, are now the most popular means of achieving a reduction in the work force, and for companies in the midst of mergers, takeovers, or downsizing, they have been one way to reduce layoffs. As times get worse, more and more companies will join firms, including such household names as AT&T, General Electric, and duPont, in trying to keep their downsizing as humane as possible. The advantages and disadvantages of the plans are very clear cut and quantifiable for employers.

In a recession, early retirement sounds particularly appealing to employees, since times are tough and there are usually no guarantees that they'll be able to keep their jobs if they don't accept the offer. The plans are fairly compelling, but on the other hand, many of these programs offer a lot less than meets the eye. To make matters worse, chances are that if you're confronted with an early-retirement incentive plan, you'll only have a month or so to evaluate the offer. You can't be too careful in assessing something that will dramatically affect the rest of your life.

What Are Your REAL Choices?

Before trying to compare working and retiring by drawing up a list of the pros and cons, or trying to project your retired versus working income and expenses for the next thirty years, you must assess your situation realistically. Do you really *have* to take the deal offered you, or do you think you still have some choices? What is the likelihood of continued employment if you decline the current offer? You're on the inside now; have you noticed anything that indicates how badly the company is being affected by the recession? If things are really bad, the incentive plan might be only the beginning of a reduction in the work force from which you will be laid off anyway, have your pay frozen or cut, or be transferred to a less desirable job. You should consider whether there already have been layoffs at the company and if so, how they were implemented. Some companies, like Digital Equipment Corporation (DEC) in Massachusetts, that have not been able to reduce their payroll sufficiently through relatively humane early-retirement options, already have started making less and less generous offers. If you're worried about your job future at the company, the early-retirement plan may well be your most palatable option. If future layoffs appear likely, you may have little choice but to participate in an early-retirement program.

One clue as to what will happen to your job if you try to keep it may be in the early-retirement offer itself. If it's limited to one plant or one department, it probably signals significant change for those who remain. If, on the other hand, the company is offering the option across the board, say to all employees over age fifty-five with over ten years of experience, your job may not be subject to future eliminations. In general, the narrower the cut, the worse it bodes for those who refuse it. If you have no choice but to take the early-retirement offer, you must plan for the future. If you have some choice, you still need to plan for the future, and your plans may influence whether or not you will take the offer.

Assuming you do have a choice and that you still enjoy working, you've got a lot of factors to weigh before making your decision. It's true that many early-retirement incentive programs look appealing at first glance; incentives may include additional or enhanced pension benefits, retiree health insurance, and lump-sum cash benefits. However, you should keep in mind that the high cost of living and the erosion of purchasing power due to inflation may make such benefits much less attractive in only a few years.

Less than Meets the Eye

To put it bluntly, most people cannot afford to retire early—even if they think they can, and even with a generous company-sponsored incentive plan. If you would like to take early retirement, you need to take a hard look at how easily you will be able to meet your living expenses, not just now, but also ten, twenty, and thirty years from now. Many employees who leave their jobs under company sponsored early-retirement plans often discover later that they won't have enough income to support themselves.

Since early retirees will probably have to finance more work-free years from their (often fixed) resources, inflation is more of an issue in determining whether pension and savings are sufficient support. If living costs increase an average of 4 percent per year, the purchasing power of a fixed retirement income will diminish by one-third after ten years and by more than half after twenty years.

Company sponsored early-retirement incentive plans often look particularly appealing because the company benefits officer shows you how much more you'll receive with the plan than if you were to quit your job now without it. However, unless you were considering retiring anyway, this isn't really a useful comparison. A better comparison would be between the package that is being offered and what you could expect if you stayed in your job as long as you originally intended. You will be sacrificing something; if you weren't, how would your company be saving money?

For example, even a beefed-up early-retirement pension is likely to be considerably smaller than the pension you could expect if you continued to work. That's because your pension is probably based on the average of what you earned in the last few years you worked. Even if the early-retirement incentive plan adds bonus years of employment and bonus years of age to your pension formula, it won't be able to make up the difference between your average salary for the last five years and your presumably higher average salary for your last five years if you were to continue working. Of course, if this recession looks like it's going to hurt your company so badly that those hypothetical future pay increases never materialize, then the difference between retiring now and retiring later shrinks.

If you're ready to quit your job anyway, and the

extra years of leisure are worth the reduced benefits, then the crucial issue for you is not how the early-retirement package compares with the normal retirement options, but whether the package is sufficient to meet your retirement income needs. To answer that you will have to project your retirement income and expenses.

Budgeting for Early Retirement

Before accepting or rejecting any window incentive plan, you must project your income and expenses until age eighty-five or ninety, taking inflation into account. The following guidelines should help you estimate some of those items more accurately. Be honest and realistic. You don't want to run out of money later.

• Many people mistakenly assume that their tax burden will lighten significantly at retirement. You will avoid some taxes, but on the other hand, taxes could go up again and cost you more than they do now. Many Washington observers are beginning to think that the 1990 tax increase is just the beginning.

• People also tend to overestimate how much their living expenses will drop. Most retirees spend 75 percent as much as they did while working, to maintain roughly the same lifestyle. Some spend more.

• One commonly overlooked expense is health insurance. Most early-retirement incentive plans extend your company health insurance coverage after you leave work. If yours doesn't, you'll have to pay high premiums for an individually purchased policy until you become eligible for Medicare at sixty-five.

• Many early retirees count on working part-time to supplement their retirement income. Part-time employment answers the two most frequent complaints of early retirees: too much time and too little money; but don't count on this option. Good part-time jobs that are financially and emotionally rewarding may not be as plentiful as you think. Right now, the economic conditions that caused your company to offer you the window incentive are also affecting your potential employers. Good full-time jobs may be even harder to find than part-time jobs. Don't simply assume you'll be able to get a full- or part-time job.

• Also, planning for part-time employment should take into account not only the additional income it produces but also the additional costs it may incur, such as higher income taxes and reduced Social Security benefits.

Other Factors to Consider

You also must weigh the effects of an early retirement on your non-company-related retirement income.

Social Security benefits. Your Social Security benefits will be reduced if you opt to collect before age sixty-five. You can receive reduced benefits after age sixty-two. Not only are the monthly checks lower, but the future cost of living increases also are proportionally lower because they are calculated from a lower initial benefit amount. As a result, benefits for early retirees will lag further and further behind inflation. Retirement beyond sixty-five, on the other hand, increases Social Security benefits by 3 percent each year that collection of benefits is postponed, until age seventy. The following table shows what percent of full Social Security benefits you will be entitled to collect if you retire at various ages.

While it still may be appropriate for you to begin drawing Social Security benefits at age sixty-two, one rule of thumb I use in advising people who are considering early retirement is: if your projections show that you will *have* to begin drawing Social Security benefits

EFFECT ON SOCIAL SECURITY BENEFITS OF EARLY AND LATE RETIREMENT

Retirement Age	Amount You Can Collect, As a Percent of Full Benefit
62	80.0%
63	86.7
64	93.3
65	100.0
66	103.0
67	106.0

at age sixty-two to help meet living expenses, you probably can't afford to retire early.

Personal retirement plans. Any funds that you have set aside to supplement your retirement pension through Individual Retirement Accounts (IRAs), Keogh or Self-Employed Pension (SEP) plans, 401(k) plans, or deferred annuities may be affected by your early-retirement decision. You will have contributed to the plans for fewer years when you retire, and you probably will begin withdrawing from the plans sooner than you would have otherwise. You generally cannot withdraw funds from personal retirement savings plans before age fifty-nine and a half without incurring a steep penalty. Even if you can afford to delay payments and avoid the penalties, there will be less available to withdraw than if you had contributed for a few more years. As a consequence of these reductions, personal savings and investments are even more crucial to early retirees than to workers who wait longer to retire. Normally, company pension plans also penalize early retirees, but the waiver of this penalty is usually the first provision of any window incentive plan.

Similar to my previous comment on Social Security, if you are likely to have to rely on your personal retirement savings plans to meet living expenses before age sixty-five, you may not be able to afford an early retirement. Distributions from a 401(k) or other company sponsored tax-deferred savings plan may be subject to a 10 percent penalty if you elect to take them before age fifty-nine and a half. Your best bet is to roll any such distributions over into an IRA within sixty days of receiving the funds, and let these funds continue to grow free of taxes until you begin withdrawing. Live off your severance and personal savings. Finally, if, as is usually the case, a large amount of your retirement income is going to be fixed—in the form of an annuity, for example—and you will not be able to save a portion of it each year to help pay increased future living costs, you may not be able to afford an early retirement. In other words, you should plan to save some of your retirement income each year.

The Brighter Side

If you've been looking forward to an early retirement that might be augmented by an early-retirement plan, the above caveats may seem discouraging. Early retirement is a very attractive prospect for many people, and the current dismal economy makes daily work life less exciting, if not downright depressing. It *is* possible to retire early and retire well, but you need to be very certain of your long-term financial security. If you have accumulated sufficient personal resources, your projections may show that you can afford an early retirement under the terms offered by your employer. You may want to ask an accountant to help you make your retirement income and expense projections. All I ask is that you be very careful and realistic in projecting your income and expenses until age ninety. If the numbers work and if you want to take early retirement, by all means do so.

IN EVALUATING AN EARLY-RETIREMENT INCENTIVE PLAN

☐ Determine how much choice you really have. What will happen to your company in the future? What will happen to your job? If the likely alternative is being fired, take the offer.

☐ If you have a choice, compare the package to the retirement benefits you would receive if you continued to work—not to those you would receive if you retired immediately without the package.

☐ Examine how you feel about your job, and consider how you would like to spend the next thirty or forty years of your life. Would you enjoy the leisure of leaving your job, or would you feel bored and restless?

☐ Project your retirement income and expenses until age ninety. The retirement benefits that look so generous now, look a lot different when you see how thirty or more years of inflation can erode your purchasing power.

☐ Determine how your other resources would be affected by an early retirement.

☐ Ascertain how long your severance pay and personal resources alone would be able to support you, so you can avoid steep penalties on early-retirement fund withdrawals and let your personal retirement accounts accumulate tax free.

☐ Examine your prospects for continuing employment realistically. If your company offers postemployment job counseling, take advantage of it.

WHAT TO DO WHEN YOUR EXPENSES ARE INCREASING FASTER THAN YOUR INCOME

I just got a notice at work today that there will be no raises this year because business is down. My wife's company has asked management to take a 10 percent pay cut. We are really feeling squeezed. Our utilities, taxes, and gasoline costs are rising by leaps and bounds, but our pay isn't. We are already dipping into savings to meet our living expenses, and it looks like our situation is going to get worse.

Millions of American workers are having to endure steadily rising living expenses although their pay is not being increased or may, in fact, be reduced. It is painful to see gasoline prices going through the roof when your take-home pay seems to be moving in the opposite direction. These days, ten dollars worth of gas barely moves the needle on your fuel gauge!

Even if you are lucky enough not to suffer any major financial disruption, such as unemployment, during the recession, you still may have difficulty making ends meet. If you find yourself fearing that your income might be frozen or simply won't keep pace with the rising costs of living, the following sections will help you minimize the discomfort.

Ways to Close the Gap When Expenses Rise Faster than Income

If your income isn't going to rise in the foreseeable future, or if it isn't rising as much as your expenses, there are actions you can take to maintain a sound financial footing. No one knows how long this recession will last, but if you heed some of the following suggestions, you will be prepared to weather the worst of it. Also, refer to Chapter Five, which offers guidance on budgeting.

• **Put your living expenses on a diet.** Although you may not want to think about it, reducing your living expenses is the best way to make ends meet when your expenses are creeping up faster than your income. At this point you probably are saying: "There is no way that I can reduce my expenses." If that's what you think, you haven't thought hard enough. Refer to Chapter Six, which lists 101 ways to reduce your living expenses.

• **Reduce your savings rate.** Another way to increase the amount of cash that you have available to meet living expenses is to reduce the amount that you save, temporarily. If you have been a regular saver up to this point, you will probably be pained by the notion of reducing your savings rate, and will restore it to its former level as soon as you can. Unless your situation is particularly precarious, try to continue saving at least a small amount each week or month. This will give you a psychological boost during an otherwise stressful time, and those savings can provide a cushion if the economic doldrums continue or worsen.

• **Find other sources of income.** In addition to, or rather than putting your expenses on a diet, you can close your fiscal deficit by fattening up your income. You may want to consider moonlighting, or if you are a homemaker, taking a part-time job to enhance household revenue. Chapter Seven describes other ways to put some extra money into your pocket.

• **Dip into savings.** Although dipping into savings to meet living expenses is a painful action to take, some people will have to do so in order to cope with strains in family finances. This action should be taken *only* after you have thoroughly and realistically examined better alternatives to weather the storm, such as reducing living expenses and finding other sources of income, as described above.

• **Borrow.** Borrowing to meet living expenses is a last resort. As explained in Chapter Eight, there are good reasons to borrow and bad reasons to borrow. One general rule of thumb for individuals, businesses, and governments is that you never borrow to meet current expenses. Just look at the federal government and the many states and cities that have borrowed to balance their budgets, only to end up in dire financial straits. Nevertheless, if you already have reduced living expenses to the bare necessities and taken other actions such as those discussed above, you may need to borrow to avert financial disaster. Don't assume that you can borrow to raise money to make ends meet, however. You may not qualify for a loan under your present circumstances. Even if you can, you may end up spending years extricating yourself from your indebtedness, much like the government.

Case Study—John and Natalie N.

The dilemma. John and Natalie N. fear they are in for some tough financial sledding. John just got word that he isn't going to get a raise this year, and his employer indicated that if business conditions don't turn around quickly, pay may be frozen for the next eighteen months. Natalie works as a part-time real estate broker, and the local real estate market stinks. This year she made $10,000, but she thinks that her income will be down almost 40 percent next year. Fortunately, John and Natalie see the handwriting on the wall and are already hard at work figuring out what they are going to do in 1991 to address the problem that millions of other families face: declining income and increasing living expenses.

• **Their plan.** John and Natalie know that their income is going to decline by $4,000 next year, and they estimate that inflation alone will increase their living expenses by $2,500. In sum, they have a total negative change in their finances for next year of $6,500 (the

---

WORK SHEET TO PLAN FOR CHANGES IN INCOME AND EXPENSES

	The Newsoms	You
Over the year, I expect my expenses to increase	$2,500	$_____
Over the next year, I expect my income to increase or (decrease)	(4,000)	_____
Shortfall—the amount that the increase in my expenses will exceed the change in my income	$6,500	$_____
I expect to meet the shortfall by:		
Reducing living expenses	$3,500	$_____
Reducing current level of savings	2,000	_____
Finding other sources of income	—	_____
Dipping into savings	1,000	_____
Borrowing	_____	_____
Total	$6,500	$_____

$4,000 decline in Natalie's income plus the $2,500 inflationary hike in expenses), assuming there are no major changes in their lifestyle. Since they have anticipated these problems, they can take action to minimize them. To avoid making matters worse, they have wisely decided to forgo any big-ticket purchases next year that would add to their expenses. For example, they wanted to trade in their five-year-old car next year for a new one, but now they agree they can put up with the old car for one more year.

But even if they postpone any big purchases, how are they going to balance the books? After a lot of studying—and some disagreement on the details—John and Natalie have decided on the following actions.

1. They will reduce their living expenses by $3,500 next year by taking a less expensive vacation, dining out less frequently, and becoming more budget conscious.

2. They are reluctantly reducing their savings level from $100 to $60 per week. This is particularly painful since the savings are earmarked to help pay tuition for their two young children, but under the circumstances, they are glad they won't have to eliminate all their savings.

3. Finally, they are going to dip into their savings accounts for the additional $1,000 necessary to balance their income and expenses. Of course, they could have accomplished the same thing by reducing their savings by another $20 per week, but they need the $1,000 immediately to pay their holiday bills.

John and Natalie's shortfall and plan of action is summarized in the work sheet. Note that there is a second column on the work sheet that provides space for you to make your own plan, should you need to.

IF YOUR EXPENSES ARE INCREASING
FASTER THAN YOUR INCOME

- ☐ Examine your finances to find ways to close the gap.
- ☐ Cutting expenses is the best way to reduce the shortfall.
- ☐ A part-time job can raise household revenue.
- ☐ Even if you have to reduce your savings level, save what you can.
- ☐ Borrowing to pay current expenses should be used only as a last resort.
- ☐ Prepare a plan that shows how you are going to make ends meet, and stick to it.

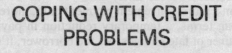

21

COPING WITH CREDIT PROBLEMS

Every day I'm getting calls from anxious creditors and collection agencies. I'm trying to pay off my bills. Don't they realize times are tough?

It is very easy to fall into the overspending and over-borrowing traps. Most of us have or can expect to fall into these traps at some point. Very few people, no matter what their income, go through life without experiencing some financial strain. In prosperity, people tend to overextend themselves, assuming that the money will keep rolling in. When the economy softens, they find that they're trying to pay for last year's excesses on this year's paycheck. You can take steps to keep anxious creditors at bay, get your debts under control, and keep overdue bills from having too adverse an effect on your life, or even on your credit rating.

The first warning sign of overindebtedness is late payments. Late payments result in late charges, which can be substantial, and can affect your credit record. Do not underestimate the gravity of late payments. If you will not be able to meet any loan payment, including your credit cards, act *before* the actual delinquency occurs, if at all possible. Explain the circumstances to the creditor. If you contact them before they are compelled to contact you, they will much more likely believe that you intend to pay off the debt, and it is much more likely that you will be able to agree on a more convenient payment date, more favorable loan terms, a temporary reduction in payments, or a waiver of late charges. As the borrower, it's up to you to meet the terms of the legal contract of the loan. If you keep the lender informed of your circumstances, however, the lender will be more inclined to amend the terms of the loan or to keep it from affecting your credit history. Do not avoid calls or letters from creditors under any circumstances. Your creditors would much rather know that you are trying to work things out, than fear that you are trying to evade the whole debt.

Keeping creditors at bay is only possible if you are honestly trying to get your financial life in order. You must commit to working out your problems.

☐ Reduce your living expenses. Chapter Six shows 101 ways to cut day-to-day expenses. Many of them should work for you.

☐ Work out an aggressive program to pay down debt, which means you'll have to go without some of the luxuries that probably got you into trouble in the first place.

☐ Prioritize your loans so that nothing important is jeopardized. If you can only afford to make the minimum payment on your credit card loan because the mortgage is due, don't miss the mortgage payment. On the other hand, if you ever have a little extra cash to spare, work down the high-interest credit card debt before paying extra against lower interest, but more important, debts.

☐ If your credit problems are particularly acute, unload some assets; for example, sell your car.

☐ Restructure your debt. Discuss payment options
with your credit counselor or creditors. Once new
terms have been agreed to, it is crucial that you
abide by them. In most cases, the restructured
debt will appear in your credit history as a delinquency even though the creditor agreed to it. This
is an excellent time to write a statement to be
included in your credit history, as is your right (see
Chapter Eight).

☐ Whatever the situation, keep the lines of communication open with your creditors.

☐ Get help from a credit counseling bureau (more on
this later).

☐ Cut up your credit cards. If you have to keep one
for identification, keep your American Express
card, because it forces you to pay off the balance
due every month.

Quick Cures to Avoid

Like many mistakes in life, the deeper you get into
debt, the harder it is to get out. Also, the deeper you
get into debt, the more vulnerable you are to any
number of schemes designed to rob you of your money
just when you need it the most. If you have credit
problems, talk to your creditors, a nonprofit credit
counseling service, or a bank officer. Do not be
tempted to fall for any of the following.

Loan sharks. Despite consumer-protection laws and
publicized warnings, as long as there are people willing
to pay exorbitant fees for borrowed money, there will
be loan sharks ready to prey on them. Loan sharks are
lenders who charge illegally high interest rates to lend
money to persons that legitimate lenders consider
below acceptable credit risk levels. No amount of

money for any purpose is worth involvement with a loan shark. Their collection techniques, although popularly exaggerated, are sometimes as far outside of the law as their interest rates. Seek credit counseling from legitimate sources; don't resort to shady operators.

Loan consolidation. This one really is tempting. The idea behind loan consolidation is that you take out one loan to cover all your debts, and then you pay only that one debt in low monthly installments spread over many years. This may well be the kind of thinking that got you into credit trouble in the first place. Lower monthly payments on any loan means that the loan is extended over a long period of time, incurring greater interest charges in total. In this case, you are incurring additional debt that will keep you in the red longer, just because it makes each payment smaller. Plus, you may be converting unsecured debt into secured debt. During the longer payoff period, it is entirely possible that you will incur new debts, bringing your monthly payments back up to the levels you previously couldn't afford. If proper loan planning is done in the first place, the need for a consolidation loan should never arise. If your monthly payments have gotten higher than you can afford, try, through credit counseling or by tightening your budgetary belt, to avoid loan consolidation. If you have no choice but to arrive at a lower monthly payment, discuss loan consolidation with a lending officer to arrive at a sensible plan that will help you out of trouble instead of keeping you in it for a longer period of time.

Credit Counseling

A nonprofit, impartial credit-counseling service, such as the National Foundation for Consumer Credit, the Consumer Credit Counseling Agency, or Family Service America, can offer assistance in how to budget expenses and pay off your debt. Your banker should be able to provide you with details about how to contact these organizations. These services can design a repayment schedule to fit your needs. Remember, however, that if you use a credit counseling service, it will go on your credit report, indicating to potential future creditors that you've had trouble managing your debt in the past. Once you, the service, and your creditors agree to a repayment schedule, you pay the service the monthly sum agreed upon for handling your bills, and it pays your creditors. These services are usually not too expensive, and often they are willing to work with people who can't afford to pay. If the counselor can't work out a repayment schedule that your creditors will accept, or decides you are too far behind ever to catch up, then you should consider filing for bankruptcy. Bankruptcy, discussed in Chapter Twenty-eight, should be considered only as a last resort. If your debt problems are chronic, contact Debtors Anonymous.

IF YOU ARE HAVING PROBLEMS HANDLING YOUR DEBTS

- ☐ Contact your creditors before they contact you.
- ☐ Work out a reasonable payment plan that your creditors agree to and that you can stick to.
- ☐ Reduce your living expenses so that you can devote more funds to getting current and reducing your debt.
- ☐ Prioritize your bills, so you don't jeopardize important assets.
- ☐ Pay off higher interest bills first.
- ☐ Tear up your credit cards.
- ☐ If necessary, seek help from a nonprofit consumer credit counseling organization.
- ☐ Stay away from loan consolidations if you possibly can.

22

ADVICE FOR HOMEOWNERS

Housing prices are declining in our neighborhood. Maybe we should have bought somewhere else. We're having some trouble making our mortgage payments every month, and we're not sure it's worth it. But what happens if we have to sell?

Housing prices have been dropping steadily in many parts of the country, fueling the fear of a national housing recession and scaring many homeowners into thinking homeownership might not be everything they'd been led to believe. If you're worried about the value of your home, remember that there's really no such thing as a national housing market and no way to make generalizations that include everyone. Housing prices are *up* in several areas of the country and they are holding steady in many others.

Homeownership *is* all it's cracked up to be. It gives you tax advantages, control over housing costs, and the security and pride of proprietorship. While you own your home, it gives you those benefits, whether or not it's appreciating in price at the moment. Capital appreciation can be a great advantage of owning a home, but it is not the only or most important advantage.

A home is a wonderful investment, but it is not a short-term one, so don't get depressed over short-term price fluctuations. Over the long run, housing prices normally do beat inflation, but if your house declines in value temporarily, don't panic. Unless you need to sell or borrow against the value of your home, changes in its paper value don't mean anything to you.

Actually, if you're committed to your house as a long-term investment, you could even take advantage of any decline in your home's value. If prices have dropped recently on homes comparable to yours, challenge your property tax assessment. Chances are it's based on an outdated appraisal, and you can have your property tax bill reduced. That's an easy way to save money on your paper losses!

Improving Your Home (Instead of Moving Out of It)

If you aren't in a hurry to leave your home, the weakened housing market may be good news for another reason. Many homeowners are finding a silver lining in the softening real estate market. Conditions for remodeling are better today than they have been in several years in many areas of the country. Once-overbooked remodeling contractors are likely to be available, eager to please, and price competitive, thanks to the slowdown in construction. Interest rates have finally declined to the point that home-equity loans and mortgage refinancings are beginning to look more feasible. If you save all your receipts, you can adjust the tax basis of your home by the amount you spent remodeling it, so when you do sell the house, your capital gains taxes could be lowered.

Remodeling your home always costs more and takes longer than you expect and shouldn't be taken up lightly. Before you initiate any substantial changes in your residence, weigh the pitfalls as well as the advantages of remodeling.

If you can't sell your home right now, but you are planning to sell it as soon as things look better, you probably shouldn't remodel first. For one thing, you can't be sure the new buyers will see your changes as improvements, and even if they do, you probably won't make up the amount you spend. Besides, extensive remodeling can be as draining as moving into a new house, because you have to live in the construction site with strangers doing the construction. If you think you'll sell soon, you'd be better off simply making sure everything works well and the house looks good. Spend your time, money, and energy cleaning out the closets so they'll look bigger or painting the kitchen a brighter color instead of renovating it. In the short term, and in this sluggish market, these little tricks will pay off, and big renovations won't. Also, no matter how long you expect to stay in the house, don't undertake any remodeling job until you have lived in the house for a few years. You'll be surprised at how much your renovation plans will change after living there for a while.

Once you decide to remodel, prepare to do a lot of planning well in advance of the actual work. One important component of ultimate financial success is to make the right kind of improvements. For example, adding a turret to house your telescope, a heart-shaped hot tub, or a boccie-ball court may make the house just perfect for you, but it won't add to its resale value.

Another common mistake is to improve beyond what your neighborhood real estate market can support. Anyone who can afford to pay extra for the swimming pool and gazebo that you add to your tract house in a middle-class area probably can afford to live in a better neighborhood. Generally, the improvements that most increase the value of your home are universally attractive enhancements, such as remodeling the kitchen, modernizing or adding a bathroom, and adding a closet or living space. Ceiling fans, energy-efficient windows and doors, and extra insulation save you money while you still own the house and recoup their value when you sell it. Swimming pools and other frivolous luxuries generally recover significantly less, and have been known to impair the resale value of a house.

While you may be able to take advantage of a slow period for the construction trades, don't try to get a bargain. The National Association of the Remodeling Industry says 80 percent of its complaints come from people who tried to buy cheap. Usually they did buy cheap—cheap materials and shoddy workmanship. Think twice before deciding to be your own general contractor. This is a time-consuming and often frustrating task, and it is usually worth the extra expense to hire a reputable contractor—after checking his or her references thoroughly.

One more crucial point: Although it would probably cost a lot less than buying a new home and selling your current home in a soft market, can you afford to remodel? Even with contractors cutting prices, it's still an expensive proposition. If you're planning on taking out a home-equity loan to cover the costs, this may not be the best time to put any additional liens on your home. Besides, in such uncertain times, you should probably be reducing your loans, not adding to them.

Refinancing

Another way that you might be able to make your current housing more attractive (by making it cheaper to own!) is to refinance your mortgage. If interest rates fall, as they often do during a recession, you may be able to refinance your mortgage at a lower rate, and many experts are predicting that rates will decline in 1991. You can save thousands of dollars by refinancing, if you stay in your home long enough to recoup the out-of-pocket costs of the refinancing. But do your homework first, because refinancing is not always the deal it seems.

Refinancing costs money, and it conceivably could end up costing you more than the new mortgage saves you. Banks usually charge a fee of 1 to 3 percent of the amount being refinanced, expressed as points. Even if that's less than the points on the original mortgage, no one's offering you a refund on those, so you'll be paying the bank twice. The bank will also expect you to pay its legal counsel, which can easily cost several hundred dollars or over $1,000. If you hire your own lawyer as well, it will double your legal bill. Other common expenses include having the house appraised, tracing the title, filing various documents, and applying for the loan (although application fees are often refundable if the loan is accepted). All these expenses add up, and they can add up to more than you'll save by refinancing.

Before you add up all the costs and calculate whether it's still worth it, you also have to determine the tax consequences of refinancing. None of the above costs are immediately deductible. Points on a first mortgage are deductible in the year paid, but deductions for points paid in refinancing must be spread out over the life of the loan. Tax considerations also narrow the monthly savings expected from the new loan. Smaller mortgage payments mean smaller tax deductions for consumer interest, so the after-tax benefit is probably smaller than it appears. So, add up all the costs and compare them with your expected savings, and if you plan to stay in your house long enough to break even, go ahead and refinance.

Selling in a Soft Market

If you can avoid selling your home in a weak market, you probably should, but if your circumstances change and you really have to sell now, or if you've really wanted to trade up and you think this is the only time you can afford to, here are some tips for making the sale as painless as possible.

Set a realistic price. If other home prices in your neighborhood have come down, yours has too. It doesn't make sense to list the house at more than it's currently worth. You won't get your price, and it'll be harder to interest brokers when you finally lower the price. Besides, buyers who notice how long the house stays on the market may wonder what's keeping it from selling and stay away from it.

Make your house stand out. At a minimal cost, you can make your house a little more memorable to prospective buyers who are tired from a long day traipsing through open houses. Clean up the whole house, even inside the closets and other storage spaces, to make it look bigger and more appealing. Keep the lawn mowed and the front yard attractively landscaped, and clean up around the front door in case the prospective buyers are standing there for a while. (Do you remember how many times you drove by your house before you bought it?) Put on a colorful bedspread, or throw a rug by the fireplace. Obviously, the new owners won't be buying your furniture, but it will affect the way they see the house.

Consider renting the old home. If you want to buy a new house while prices are low, consider renting your current one instead of selling it right away—if you can afford to buy the new home without selling the old one. The rental income will help you carry the costs of two homes, and you can wait until housing prices improve to sell the old one.

Foreclosure

No matter how prepared you think you are, the recession could change your financial circumstances so much that it becomes hard to make your mortgage payments. If you start having difficulties or anticipate that you may soon, start planning immediately so that you can avoid foreclosure and keep your home. As with any credit trouble, contact the lender as soon as you anticipate a problem (see Chapter Twenty-one). In these rough times, many mortgage lenders are going out of their way to help distressed homeowners keep their homes. They don't do this out of the kindness of their hearts, but because foreclosure is a long and expensive process, during which they don't get any payments. Besides, by the time they assume control of the property, it usually needs repairs. Lenders often wind up losing a substantial portion of the original mortgage on a foreclosure. They'd much rather work out some way to avoid that. When they rework a loan, they frequently don't lose a thing, and the owners get to keep their home.

Banks generally lose in a foreclosure, but what about you? Houses are losing value so fast in some areas, that many homeowners find they owe the bank more than the house is now worth! Some homeowners are tempted to abandon the mortgage and mail the bank the keys. But, unfortunately, it isn't that easy. The mortgage you signed is a legal document, which binds you to pay the debt no matter what. A foreclosure goes on your credit record for seven years. It can make it very difficult to get credit, and it can also impair the credit you already have. Many credit card lenders and holders of other unsecured debt review your credit report from time to time. While some will base your standing with them only on how you pay their bills, others will lower your credit limit, take away your card, or refuse to renew your card if they spot a foreclosure, even if you're paid up with them.

In addition, there's no guarantee that the bank can get back the value of the mortgage when they sell your house. If you don't repay them the difference, they may be able to seize your car, other assets, or savings, or garnishee your paychecks for as long as twenty years. Not all states allow such "deficiency judgments," but as real estate values drop, more and more will. If the bank can't force you to repay the difference between the auction price of the house and the outstanding debt, the IRS will step in. They consider any shortfall "forgiveness of debt," meaning a payment from the lender to you, and you'll have to pay taxes on that payment.

Your mortgage is your most important bill. Try to pay it, even if it means falling behind in other areas. But if you can't, you can't. If that's the case, contact the bank. They'll try to arrange what's known as a "workout," a plan to work out the situation. Your workout probably will not lower the amount you owe, but it might change your payment schedule so you can make lower payments now and make up for it later. Other workout arrangements include changing from an adjustable-rate to a fixed-rate mortgage or extending the length of the loan so you can make up for missed payments. If you can't agree on a workout, some lenders and mortgage insurance companies will help you sell your home—even if it won't bring in enough to pay them off. If you owe the bank more money than the sale raises, and you absolutely can't pay the balance, the bank may grant you an interest-free loan. Obviously, the bank doesn't want to do that, but they usually still lose less that way than in a foreclosure.

Many banks are beginning to train their staff on crisis debt counseling, and they want to help. If your problems are temporary, contact your lender early and present a timely plan for repayment. When you go to the bank, bring, in writing:

- your personal and business tax returns;
- a summary of your assets, including retirement plans, life insurance, and investments; and
- a summary of your liabilities, including car payments, credit card payments, and medical bills.

The bank may be able to work out a plan with your other lenders, and it will try to help you keep your home—and help them keep their loan.

TIPS FOR HOMEOWNERS DURING TOUGH TIMES

- ☐ If you don't need to sell, don't worry about your paper losses. Your home provides you with a lot more than capital appreciation, and if you can ride out this recession, it'll probably provide you with that too.
- ☐ There is no national housing market, only local markets. Don't assume things are bad where you are just because you hear they're bad somewhere else.
- ☐ A home is a long-term commitment. Don't overreact to short-term events.
- ☐ If you can't sell your home without taking a loss, consider improving it instead.
- ☐ Practical home improvements often add value to your home, but if you add something frivolous, don't expect to recoup your investments when you sell.
- ☐ If you're worried about the economy, don't take out further loans on the house.

☐ If you're going to stay in your house for a while, you might be able to reduce costs by refinancing your mortgage if interest rates decline in 1991.

☐ If you have to sell your house in a soft market, price it realistically, and do what you can to make it attractive to prospective buyers.

☐ If you want to buy a new house while prices are down, but you don't want to sell the old one, consider renting the old home until prices recover, but *only* if you can afford to carry two mortgages indefinitely.

☐ If you are having or anticipate having trouble making your mortgage payments, talk to the lender about ways to avoid foreclosure. They can help only if you ask them.

23

GETTING THE KIDS THROUGH COLLEGE DURING BAD TIMES

We always promised our children that if they studied hard they could go to college wherever they wanted. We started saving for tuition when they were still in the cradle. Now that the time's getting close, I'm afraid we can't afford to keep our promise. Tuition seems unreasonably expensive. Don't colleges know there's a recession?

It has *never* been easy to get children through college, but for many parents, it's going to be even harder during the recession for a number of reasons.

- Tuition costs have consistently outpaced inflation for several decades, but in more prosperous times, most parents could expect their income at least to keep pace with inflation. During a recession, costs will continue to rise, and college costs will definitely continue to rise even faster, but *parents can no longer assume their income will keep pace*. Right now, tuition costs are rising at a 7–8 percent annual rate. Most parents' incomes aren't.

- Although tuition costs are always too steep for many parents, when the economy is expanding, many government agencies and private organizations are ready to help out deserving scholars. The schools themselves have more money to distribute and fewer students who need it. Now, however, federal and state cutbacks have reduced the amount and availability of financial aid. Private aid programs are flooded with applicants, and colleges and universities are needing more and more of their available funds to meet the needs of enrolled students, decreasing the amount available to new applicants.

- Many students who do manage to find sufficient aid sources will complete their years in academia with heavy debt burdens and emerge into a job market too soft to guarantee them a livelihood, much less a means of repaying their debts.

If you're the parent of a college-bound teen, the last thing you need to hear is why it's so hard to pay tuition costs. You're probably a lot more interested in how to pay for tuition and what steps you can take to make it easier. I assure you that it *is* possible to meet rising tuition costs, although I can't promise that price won't be an issue in choosing a school. Many schools still have "need-blind" admissions policies, but that doesn't mean they're going to hand you full tuition. You should start planning and saving to meet college costs as soon as you can, but if you still fall short, many sources of assistance are available.

The Financial Aid Process

There is a common misconception that once you fill out all the forms, the government or the school of your choice decides how much aid you qualify for. Actually, you send one financial aid application to a central office, and computers calculate how much your family can afford to pay, *not* how much aid to give you. This means that you will be expected to pay the same amount no matter where your children go to school, and that amount is probably more than you think you can afford. The government and the college will pay some, but not necessarily all, of the rest. You will be able to make up the difference through a combination of grants, loans, and student employment. If your financial situation deteriorates just before your child enters college, or while he or she is enrolled, don't despair. You will be able to qualify for more financial aid, as explained later in this chapter.

Grants. Most schools will meet a high percentage of the shortfall between what the government thinks you can afford and what they cost. In addition to the amount the admissions and financial aid office offers you, the school may offer alternative sources of aid. Colleges usually offer a few scholarships that aren't based on need; ask about them early, in case they require a separate application. You may be able to discover other sources of aid—from alumni groups, the student affairs office, or the individual academic or athletics departments. Math, science, and engineering departments tend to have the most money, while the humanities are notoriously poor. Off campus, some states provide grants or loans to students headed for in-state colleges.

High school counselors and college financial aid offices can help you explore these rapidly changing aid sources. There are, however, two information sources you should never use. Don't rely on what your friends say about college financial aid matters. Conditions change so rapidly that the tips they give are probably out of date. Don't pay $50 to $250 to a computerized scholarship-search service if you can get the same information free from your child's high school.

Loans. Loans are becoming the largest part of available aid, and graduates spend years repaying their debts. Many colleges won't provide students with enough financial aid to meet 100 percent of their tuition costs. Generally, parents meet the remaining gap through loans, and students get employment. Since education costs rise so fast, loans represent an increasingly large proportion of total funding. Several parent- and student-loan programs are available to fill this gap.

- **Stafford Loans (formerly Guaranteed Student Loans).** If your child chooses to attend a college whose cost is greater than your assessed family contribution, you should be eligible for a federal Stafford Loan, which allows freshmen and sophomores to borrow up to $2,625 per year, and junior and seniors up to $4,000. The interest rate is 8 percent for the first four years and 10 percent after that.
- **Parent Loans to Undergraduate Students (PLUS).** The government is willing to lend parents of college students up to $4,000 per year, regardless of financial need. The interest rate is 3.75 percentage points above the 52-week Treasury bill rate, with a 12 percent cap.
- **Supplemental Loan to Students (SLS).** This loan is similar to the PLUS, except that the government lends the money directly to the student. The terms and limits are the same as for the PLUS.

Student employment. Gone are the days when anyone could work his or her way through college. However, most college financial aid offices will expect a student to contribute toward tuition costs. Schools expect students to contribute $900 per year and will want 70 percent of your child's part-time earnings above that, not including income from work-study programs.

How to Qualify for More Aid

If you aren't sure whether your family will qualify for financial aid, apply anyway. Why not? You certainly wouldn't turn down any help the government felt like giving you, and you have to apply for federal aid to be eligible for other grants, loans, and work-study programs from the colleges. Besides, no matter how many colleges your son or daughter is applying to, you probably only have to fill out one financial aid application. Before you do, however, there are a few things you can do that may increase the amount of aid you will receive. These tips may come in particularly handy if you are being squeezed financially during the recession.

Reduce your child's assets. The government expects the student to devote 35 percent of his or her assets to paying tuition costs, but it only expects parents to use around 5–6 percent of theirs. This is one of the main arguments against giving money to minor children to save taxes. The Uniform Gifts to Minors Act prohibits you from transferring money from your child's account to your own. Instead, have the child buy any expensive supplies he or she will need for college, like a car or a computer, out of his or her own money—before you fill out the financial aid forms. If you've already filled out your aid application, have the child pay for freshman year, which could increase the amount of aid he or she will receive in later years.

Reduce your assets. Don't give money away, thinking the government will give you more, but if you're already considering a large purchase, make it now, as long as it doesn't jeopardize your financial security, especially during the economic slowdown. For every $1,000 you take out of your savings, the amount you're expected to contribute toward college costs decreases by over $50.

Restructure your debt. Consumer loans do not count as liabilities on the financial aid forms, but home-equity loans do. If you can, pay off your automobile loans, credit card debt, and other bills, so that the amount of cash you have left gives a more accurate picture of your situation. If you can't afford to pay off all your debts now, consider taking out a home-equity loan to pay them off instead of letting them ride.

Value your assets conservatively. If you own a home, its value may have dropped, due to declining real estate prices in many areas of the country. Your latest tax assessment may overstate your home's true value.

What to Do if Things Get Worse

Colleges and universities abide by the government's assessment of your financial situation. This assessment is based primarily on your tax return and other information you give them about your financial situation over the last year. However, in difficult times, it isn't uncommon for a parent's situation to worsen suddenly, and render the agreed level of aid inadequate or the agreed parental contribution unattainable.

Many families count on borrowing against their home or other assets to meet college costs in a crunch, if their circumstances are temporarily impaired. However, the recession may foil their good intentions, for three reasons.

1. The real estate market is so soft in many areas, and investment values have declined so much, that many parents' assets aren't worth what they once were.

2. Many parents' circumstances are changed to the point where they can't qualify for a loan.

3. Parents who were willing to sell their houses or other assets in an emergency are now confronted with a decaying buyer's market.

Financial aid offices are already facing a growing number of such crises. They assure me that although times are tough, there is assistance available to parents in difficult financial situations.

Short-term financial assistance. For one thing, there is a special application process for the Pell Grant program that lets the financial aid office evaluate the financial situation of the family *right now*. This can be done between school years or even in the middle of the academic year. If the student or his or her parents write to the financial aid office, or explains the change in circumstances in person, the aid office will take the change into consideration. Usually, it will be able to provide the student more campus-based aid or allow him or her to qualify for work-study programs to see the student through the current academic year, until the family can revise its status with the government.

Supplemental loans. Parents whose changed circumstances will prevent them from meeting the year's education costs can apply for supplemental loans from the government or private institutions. However, their financial duress may result in their being turned down for the loan. If the parents are denied, the student can get an SLS loan (described above) without reference to the parents' credit standing. Clearly, this is a bit of good news for students whose parents have been hit particularly hard. Students should use supplemental loans as a stopgap measure and reapply to the government as soon as they can, as they presumably will qualify for more aid.

Financial aid offices nationwide stand ready to help you through your tough times. You should consult with them as quickly, honestly, and specifically as you can. They are on your side.

PUTTING KIDS THROUGH COLLEGE IN A RECESSION

- ☐ Apply for financial aid if you have any chance of qualifying for it. Any financial aid will come in handy.
- ☐ Compare interest rates on available student loans. Government loan sources usually offer the lowest rates.
- ☐ Take legitimate steps to reduce the amount of tuition the government will expect your family to afford.
- ☐ If your financial situation deteriorates suddenly, consult with the college financial aid office about additional aid.
- ☐ College financial aid offices are ready to deal with the recession. With their help, you can too!

24

OPPORTUNITIES FOR
FIRST-TIME HOME BUYERS

*We've been saving for a home for ages, but now
we're not sure if we should buy. The economy is too
messed up, interest rates are too high, and everyone
says the real estate market has no place to go but
down. Maybe we'd be better off keeping our money
in the bank.*

It's scary to think about making a major purchase and
taking on a big financial commitment in uncertain
economic circumstances. What happens if you lose
your job and can't meet the mortgage payments? How
will your house fare as an investment?

Nobody can answer those questions for you, but
nobody could in a boom market either. Boom market
or recession, you still have to save for the down
payment, become familiar with the local real estate
market, and put your overall finances in good order so
you can qualify for a mortgage, just as you would at
any time. If you're afraid you might need the money
you've saved for a house in case you lose your job or
undergo other financial duress during the recession, or
you're afraid to commit to thirty years of monthly

mortgage payments, then perhaps now is not the time to buy. But if you have saved enough for a down payment, and the rest of your finances are relatively well braced for the recession (see Chapters Two and Three), now may be the perfect time to take advantage of a declining housing market. True, interest rates may be coming down, and housing prices might come down even further. Don't wait around for those things to happen, however. People who wait for ideal conditions usually become permanent renters. It's not worth worrying about timing the exact moment to take the plunge. Prices are low now in many areas, and if interest rates drop significantly, you can always refinance your mortgage.

Why Buy?

Buying a home is one of the best things you can do to achieve financial independence. For most people, the advantages of owning far outweigh the disadvantages.

Control over housing costs. Even if your monthly mortgage payments seems impossibly high at first, your earnings will probably increase, and your mortgage payments probably won't. Ask anyone who's owned a home for many years what their mortgage payments are—whether they bought in a recession or they bought when interest rates seemed high. Rent increases, on the other hand, usually *outpace* inflation.

Tax benefits. The tax reforms of the 1980s curtailed the tax advantages of many investments—but not primary residences. Interest on your first mortgage remains deductible on your federal income tax return, as do property taxes.

Inflation hedge. Real estate has been a solid investment over the last few inflationary decades. True, the value of your home may decrease at times. Mostly it appreciates in value, and when it does, you benefit—not your landlord. You don't even have to set your sights very high on a first home. Most first-time home buyers start out in a home and neighborhood that aren't quite as nice as the ones they grew up in, but as your house appreciates and you begin to prosper when the economy revives as it surely will, eventually you'll be able to trade up. For now the important thing may be to get into that first home.

Retirement cushion. Buying a home while you're young can be a big help at retirement. By the time you retire, you'll probably either have paid off your entire mortgage, or your payments will be very low in comparison with your income. You'll be able to use your retirement income to enjoy life, rather than making increasing rent payments. Or if you choose, you can sell your home at retirement, and use the proceeds of the sale to purchase a less expensive house outright or provide additional funds to assure a comfortable retirement. You can bet that retired people who own their homes free and clear are fretting a lot less about the effects of the recession on their pocketbooks than others with high housing costs.

Why Buy Now?

This isn't necessarily a bad time to be buying a home. The recession already has resulted in declining housing prices in many areas of the country where housing costs had been rising sharply and steadily, creating a buyers' market. If you have the money to make a downpayment, and you're reasonably sure that your income won't be hurt too much by the recession, now could be the time to buy. As times get tougher, plenty of sellers are willing to negotiate. You also may be able to take advantage of some unusual situations, such as the following.

Buying at auction. As the real estate slump spreads across the nation, home auctions are becoming increasingly common. Once used almost exclusively to unload foreclosed farm properties, auctions are used more and more as a marketing tool by real estate developers. They aren't limited to distress sales, and they're no longer limited to farms—they're becoming common in suburbs and in big cities. Buyers also may be able to secure below-market rate financing through lenders engaged by the developer.

Home auctions are usually advertised in newspapers several weeks before they occur. Call or write for a brochure describing the properties offered, and get to the auction early, because any changes the auctioneer announces, in the property description or lot size, for example, are legally binding—even if you arrive too late to hear them.

Read all the terms of the auction, so you'll know what you're getting yourself into and whether you can back out of a sale later. Auctions can be great opportunities for first-time home buyers, but don't just assume that if it's up for auction, it's a great deal. Do enough research to find out how much the properties are really worth and whether you would really want any of them. Definitely visit the property, and if you're serious about it, bring along an appraiser or other expert. Also, figure out how much you realistically can afford to pay, and stick to that limit no matter how frantic the bidding. A house can be a great deal for what it's worth and still not be the right house for you.

Buying at auction doesn't mean you'll be able to snatch a few penthouses for a few pennies. Well-advertised and well-run auctions produce large crowds of frantic bidders. Opening bids typically start at 30 to 40 percent of the original price, and many properties are bid up to market value. Even when the house sells for a fraction of its original value, that may no longer be equal to its current market value, so the buyer's discount is exaggerated. Many developers offer only a small block of units "absolute," meaning they'll accept the winning bid no matter how small it is. Otherwise, they offer the properties with a reserve option, which gives them the right to reject the winning bid, even if it exceeds the minimum bid price advertised before the auction. The developers also can call off the auction if their properties aren't fetching adequate prices. Finally, buying foreclosed property at auction can be a minefield. For example, you may not be guaranteed clear title when you buy the property, or the house may be in poor condition. To avoid potential problems, you should consult with a lawyer and home inspector *before* bidding at the auction.

Buying from the RTC. The Resolution Trust Corporation (RTC) has control over 20,000 foreclosed homes around the country, and is selling them at distressed prices; many sell for around 85 percent of their appraised value. That's a great discount for a first-time home buyer, but it's a far cry from the stories of investors snapping up mansions for a few dollars. You can't buy a house without paying for it in any market, but you may get some help in this one. A real estate broker or bank asset-sales officer should be able to provide you with information on RTC and other foreclosed properties in your area. Be prepared to deal with a complex bureaucracy if you're going to buy through the RTC.

Other distress situations. You may be able to purchase foreclosed property through a local real estate broker before it reaches the auction block. Repossessed property from failed S&Ls, the Department of Veterans Affairs, the Department of Housing and Urban Development, and other government agencies also may be listed at brokers' offices (or available directly through the agencies) before they go up for auction.

You still can buy the property at a discount, but you'll have more time to look it over and think about it. One advantage of buying from the government: You may be able to buy the property with a lower downpayment. The Federal National Mortgage Association (Fannie Mae), for example, accepts 3 percent down from owner-occupants and 10 percent down from investors for foreclosed properties, although it requires 5 and 30 percent down, respectively, from the same type of buyers for nondistress homes.

State programs for low- and moderate-income home-buyers. You may be able to qualify for state programs that facilitate homeownership for low- and moderate-income families. Some programs are structured as rent-to-own arrangements, others involve renovating the home yourself. These programs vary considerably from state to state, so check to see what's available in your state. In spite of increased fiscal pressures on the states, most of these programs are still being offered.

Financing Your New Home

If you currently or soon expect to have enough money to make a downpayment on a new home without jeopardizing your emergency reserves; if your job is secure; and if you're pretty sure you can make your mortgage payments even if you don't get a raise; then qualifying for a mortgage shouldn't be too hard. Obviously, credit is getting tighter and lenders are getting stricter, so don't be surprised if they make you produce reams of paperwork prior to granting the mortgage. But remember, fewer people will be applying, and fewer of them will have your qualifications. If you try diligently, and you have been disciplined in your personal financial planning, you will get the mortgage.

But what kind of mortgage should you get? *Adjustable-rate mortgage (ARM)* rates are particularly attractive during a recession because they're normally tied to yields on short-term securities; and in tough economic times and times of international tension, investors tend to pile into short-term securities, holding rates steady or even driving them down. Since the onset of the Persian Gulf crisis, for example, ARM rates have held relatively steady, and fixed rates have steadily climbed.

On the other hand, *fixed-rate mortgages* seem pretty attractive if interest rates start to climb in a few years. If you can get a fixed-rate mortgage at under 10 percent, take it. If you fear a long period of high inflation, which most experts aren't predicting, get a fixed-rate mortgage, and control your housing costs while other expenses rise. Otherwise, stick with a variable-rate mortgage. You can always refinance later.

RECESSION OPPORTUNITIES FOR FIRST-TIME HOME BUYERS

- ☐ If your job and financial prospects are secure, you may be able to take advantage of a declining housing market.
- ☐ Do not abandon the goal of homeownership in a recession. Do set your sights realistically.
- ☐ During a recession, you may be able to buy a home at less than its market value through auctions, foreclosures, and other special circumstances, but you must learn the procedures and the pitfalls.
- ☐ Even moderate-income people should find out if they are eligible for any state programs that facilitate homeownership.
- ☐ Obtaining financing is possible in spite of a tight credit market.

☐ ARMs look attractive, but if you expect high inflation or can get a rate under 10 percent, consider a fixed-rate mortgage.

25

TIPS FOR WORRIED RETIREES

This recession has me scared to death. I'm like most retirees and live on a fixed income. My investments keep dropping in value, and I'm starting to hear that inflation may be rising. Who knows what's going to happen to the economy? All I can say is that it looks like old folks are going to take it on the chin.

A lot of media attention focuses on how the economy affects working people and businesses. Yet many retirees suffer every bit as much from an economic downturn as other age groups.

• Millions of retirees live on incomes that are mostly fixed, and may actually decline during the recession, while living expenses continue to increase inexorably.

• The ever-present danger of rising inflation could thrust many retirees into a precarious financial position.

• Many retirees who rely on income from their own investments to meet living expenses have found that their investments have been hurt by the turbulent stock and bond markets.

Making Ends Meet in 1991

If you are retired, the following may describe your situation. You have always worried about your ability to meet the steadily increasing costs of living on a relatively fixed income, and the recent oil problems have heightened your concern. You don't have a luxurious lifestyle, and sharp increases in the cost of oil as well as some other essentials are really beginning to concern you. As if this isn't bad enough, you've found that your investments, like everyone else's, have been performing rather poorly. Social Security increases never quite seem to keep pace with inflation, and if you're fortunate enough to have a pension plan that is adjusted for inflation from time to time (at the discretion of the pension manager), you suspect that it may be quite a while before you get the next increase.

If you are feeling squeezed, your situation is not very different from that of many working Americans. But there are a couple of big differences. The good news is that your pension and Social Security incomes are far more secure than wage income; millions of working Americans fear, and justifiably so, that the current recession may cause them to lose their jobs, and hence, their income. The bad news is that you don't have as much flexibility to increase your income or reduce your living expenses as younger people have. Nevertheless, you should be planning for the difficult times ahead in much the same way that working-age people should. Even though you may not think that you can reduce expenses, you probably can if you need to. Chapter Five provides some guidance on preparing budgets for tough economic times, and Chapter Six lists 101 ways to reduce living expenses. If reducing your expenses is not enough, then you probably need to consider increasing your income. You may be pleasantly surprised to find that there are part-time work opportunities available for able-bodied retirees. Many companies that cut back on the number of full-time employees will be seeking lower-cost, part-time help to perform needed tasks. So, don't just assume that because you are retired you have no employment prospects. Start looking around, and consult your local or state council on aging or elder affairs department. Chapter Seven lists other ways to increase your income in addition to part-time work.

The keys to coping with the current financial malaise are to plan ahead, take reasonable, well-thought-out actions to meet your current and future financial needs, and avoid doing anything drastic to your finances without consulting first with experienced and trustworthy professionals and family members.

Coping with Inflation

High inflation can be devastating to retired people with fixed incomes. You may recall that annual inflation reached the double digits in 1979 through 1981. Even under current, more moderate inflation rates—the cost of living increased a little less than 5 percent per year during the 1980s—everyone will likely see their purchasing power cut in half every fourteen years or so. Many economists note that preconditions which contribute to higher inflation are beginning to appear, and that the current recession could be accompanied or followed by a period of higher inflation. If signs start pointing to inflation, start planning for it now.

Prepare inflation budgets. Just as you should prepare a budget for the next year or so, which takes into account the immediate effects of the recession, you should also consider preparing a forecast of your expenses and income that assumes higher inflation. For example, you might assume that your living expenses will rise by 10 percent over each of the next three years. Then estimate how much, if at all, your income will increase over the same period. While most of your income may not increase with inflation, Social Security will be adjusted for inflation, although it will lag somewhat. By preparing projections and planning ahead, you will be better able to anticipate the adjustment you may have to make in order to cope with a period of higher inflation, if and when it occurs.

Hedge against inflation in your personal investments. If you, like most retirees, rely on income from your personal investments to help pay for living expenses, some of these investments must provide you with the opportunity to beat inflation. The two investment categories that provide the most consistent—albeit erratic—inflation-beating returns are real estate and stocks. Many retirees feel that these investments should be avoided because they are risky. Certainly, the 1990 performance of real estate and stocks amply illustrates the risk. On the other hand, over the long-term, stocks and real estate have provided a much higher return than the third major category of investment, interest-earning securities.

This is not to suggest that you should go out and sell your CDs and buy a lot of stocks next week. On the other hand, although it is difficult to generalize, a retiree's investment portfolio that does not include any stock is likely to suffer from the erosive effects of inflation—not this year and not the next, but ten and twenty years hence, when inflation will seriously erode the purchasing power of a fixed income. The fact is that retirees are living long and active lives today. For example, if you refer to joint life expectancy tables, a couple, both age sixty-five, have a "last to die" life expectancy of twenty-five years. In other words, on average, one of them will live to age ninety, and that is just the average. I hope that you will beat the average, but in so doing, you will need to keep your eye on how inflation is going to affect you. You can't rely on your *income* to increase along with inflation through annual raises as you did during your working years. Instead, you have to rely on your *investments* to grow with inflation, in addition to providing you with adequate interest and dividend income. Additional suggestions on investing in tough economic times appear at the end of this chapter and in several other chapters of this book.

Continue saving. One of the biggest mistakes some retirees make early in their retirement years is spending all their income. They fail to realize that they still need to save for the future so that they can have a steadily increasing income throughout their retirement years to offset steadily rising living costs. Inflation doesn't go away when you're retired. As time passes, you will need more income just to stay even. So, another way to protect against inflation is to continue saving some of your income.

Managing Your Investments

It's tough enough at any age to manage your investments effectively, but it's particularly so during your retirement years. When you were younger, you could make some investment mistakes because you had many years to make up for them. Most retirees, on the other hand, can't afford to make serious investment mistakes. Their time horizon is, of course, shorter, and they often have to rely on the income from their investments to meet current living expenses. Investing in the current environment is downright scary for retirees—and everyone else, for that matter. My feeling is that if you take a sensible, long-term approach to investing, you won't be affected too adversely during bad investment markets and you will flourish during good investment markets. Some general suggestions appear below. Refer also to Part III of this book, which discusses investing under the current difficult conditions.

Maintain a balanced portfolio that is appropriate to your needs. As I've discussed, it's important to have at least some inflation-beating investments in your portfolio, namely stocks. Real estate also provides that opportunity, but most retirees do not want to get involved in real estate investing—with the exception of the family home—because it cannot be turned into cash very quickly, should the need arise. Excluding real estate, a balanced portfolio should consist of both interest-earning investments and stock investments. Generally, retirees should have a higher proportion of their savings invested in interest-earning investments than would younger people. But as I have mentioned, stock still belongs in most retirees' investment portfolios. Typically, retired investors should invest in high-quality stocks with good dividend-paying records. High-quality stocks make particularly good sense in the current frightening stock market environment, because well-established companies with the capacity to pay generous, regular dividends will not be as adversely affected by a declining market as other stocks.

As far as interest-earning investments are concerned, retirees who pay attention to prevailing interest rates can be well rewarded. Over the past several years, and 1990 was no exception, interest rates periodically became quite attractive. What is attractive? If the yield on the bellwether thirty-year Treasury bond approaches or exceeds 9 percent, many experts feel that yields from intermediate and longer term interest-earning securities are quite attractive.

If, however, you expect that inflation is going to heat up, you will want to keep your interest-earning investments in shorter-term securities, such as money market accounts, Treasury bills, and certificates of deposit. Thus, part of your strategy for investing in interest-earning securities should be based on your own opinion of the future of the economy. If you are not very optimistic, concentrate on shorter-term securities. Often, as in all areas of personal financial planning, doing a little bit of both is the best solution. In other words, invest in some short-term as well as some longer-term securities.

Don't do anything precipitous in response to market uncertainty. Sometimes, senior citizens get themselves into financial trouble because they react too hastily to unfavorable investment market conditions. In other words, they may make a major change in their investments, often at the suggestion of some self-anointed expert. Certainly, you are concerned about keeping your money safe amidst economic uncertainty and volatile investment markets. But that doesn't mean, for example, selling all the stocks you've owned for years—thereby probably incurring capital-gains tax—and reinvesting the proceeds in CDs. If you're so frightened that you want to concentrate your investments in safer securities, fine, but do so gradually. On the other hand, you may feel that you have invested too conservatively, or perhaps, that stocks have been beaten down so badly that they are attractive. Fine, but change your investments gradually over a period of months or even a year or two. That way, you won't suffer unduly if you guess wrong. And since most experts guess wrong most of the time, it is always possible that you may do so as well.

Speaking of acting hastily, some elderly parents give all or most of their money to their children, so they won't have to use it to pay for the uninsured costs of going to a nursing home, due to Medicare limitations. As the recession deepens, more elderly people will become concerned about losing their money, and more children will be happy to relieve their parents of their money. Good luck to the parents who later try to get that money back from the children when they need it.

Don't make inappropriate investments. Just as you have to maintain a balanced portfolio that consists of a variety of carefully selected investments, you also need to avoid making risky investments. Unfortunately, retired people are favorite targets for opportunistic or unethical investment advisors, who recommend overly risky or otherwise inappropriate investments. For example, a widow I know was advised by her stockbroker to place a substantial portion of her investments in real estate deals that ended up becoming worthless. Some major firms are encouraging retirees to purchase long-term portfolios of interest-earning investments called "unit investment trusts" on the basis of the income they provide. Unfortunately, these firms downplay the fact that the unit trusts may be difficult to sell, and if they can be sold, will decline in value if interest rates rise. The best way to avoid making inappropriate investments is to stick with old-fashioned, plain-vanilla investments that you understand. If someone who is trying to sell you an investment can't describe it to your satisfaction in one sentence, don't buy it.

Be particularly careful of high-yield investments. Far too many senior citizens have been burned over the past years by junk bonds or junk-bond mutual funds. Don't be a yield chaser. Opt instead for high-quality interest-earning investments. The current economic situation is hardly the time to invest your money in securities that pay unusually high returns. There is a reason why companies pay those returns, and it isn't because they like you a lot, it's because they are riskier.

Other Tips to Help You Survive a Scary Economy

Maintain your health insurance. If you really begin to feel a financial pinch, you may be tempted to save money by dropping your health insurance, but this is penny wise and pound foolish. Always, always maintain your health insurance coverage. For persons age sixty-five an over, this usually means keeping a Medicare Gap insurance policy in force, which will protect you against incurring many large health-care bills. It is essential to keep this coverage.

Beware of scamsters. The charlatans of the world love to prey on the elderly. The current uncertain economy provides these opportunists with the perfect environment in which to operate. So be particularly wary of any investments that seem too good to be true, because they are. Also be on guard for the usual areas where you can be taken advantage of, such as attempts to sell you inappropriate, multiple health or life insurance policies, phony home improvement schemes, and anything sold over the phone. The list goes on and on. This is hardly the time to be defrauded out of one single cent.

Keep abreast of the many programs for senior citizens. Be sure to take advantage of any money-saving opportunities available to senior citizens in your local community and elsewhere. You also may be able to receive financial information from any of a variety of organizations that represent the elderly, including the American Association of Retired Persons and your local or state council on aging. There are a great number of valuable and money-saving opportunities, but it is up to you to uncover them.

Don't hesitate to seek advice. Many retirees are going to be hurt by this recession, and many more will be hurt if inflation heats up. If you are very troubled by your expected future financial situation, or if you are already experiencing financial problems, by all means don't hesitate to seek the advice of qualified professionals or family members. They may be able to help allay your fears, provide a plan that will help you cope with your financial problems, or provide other needed guidance. How do you find experienced and trustworthy financial advisors? Don't go to the yellow pages. Ask your acquaintances, banker, or family lawyer for a recommendation. As with all financial advisors, word-of-mouth referral is the best way to assure that you get the quality advice that you deserve.

One final note: I have found that far too many retirees skimp during their retirement years so that they can pass their money on to their children. I am obviously in favor of saving during your retirement years, as my previous remarks indicated, but I am also in favor of living it up when you're retired, to the extent that you can afford to. Don't worry about passing anything onto your children. Instead, try to devise a plan that will allow you to spend your children's inheritance during your lifetime. Your children may not appreciate my telling you this, but I'm a lot more concerned about you having an enjoyable retirement than I am about them receiving an inheritance. Heaven only knows what they'll do with it, anyway.

IF YOU'RE RETIRED AND YOU'RE WORRIED ABOUT HOW THE CURRENT ECONOMY WILL AFFECT YOU

- ☐ Evaluate how rising costs and declining investment markets will affect you over the next year.
- ☐ If you find that you may have trouble making ends meet, start planning to take action that will help alleviate your financial strain.

☐ If you are concerned that the rate of inflation will increase, prepare an assumed high-inflation budget to see how you would be affected.

☐ Make sure your personal investments include securities that act as a hedge against inflation, typically stocks.

☐ Continue saving when you are retired to assure that your income will rise in later years to offset the effects of higher living costs.

☐ Maintain a balanced personal investment portfolio that includes appropriate portions of interest-earning investments and stock investments.

☐ Never make any quick, major changes in your personal investment portfolio.

☐ Don't be cajoled into making inappropriate investments.

☐ Always maintain your health insurance, typically Medicare Gap insurance.

☐ Be on guard for scam artists; they're everywhere.

☐ Take advantage of cost-saving and service programs for senior citizens.

☐ Don't hesitate to seek the advice of family members or experienced professionals about your financial problems.

SURVIVAL TACTICS FOR SMALL BUSINESS OWNERS

My friends who work for giant corporations are complaining about how the recession is affecting their personal finances. I wish I had their problems. My business is going through a terrible time. Receivables are way up, I can't move the inventory, and now the bank that has the business loans is starting to get antsy. I've never experienced such a sudden drop-off in business.

Small business owners face a double whammy during a recession. They have to keep both their business and their personal finances afloat. A big risk that small business owners face in a slowdown is that they will jeopardize their personal resources in an attempt to keep the business going. If that action fails, they could end up in serious financial trouble. Many business owners don't see their personal financial life as being separate from the business, even in the best of circumstances. When push comes to shove, they gladly will sell their personal investments, borrow against their homes, and co-sign additional business loans to keep the business going. The risk of doing this is obvious, but small business owners are inherently risk takers anyway.

The next section will discuss some strategies that may help you cope with the financial problems that plague many businesses during a slowdown. It is followed by a discussion of the inevitable interrelationship between the finances of the business and the personal finances of its owner.

Taking Care of Business

One key to dealing effectively with the recession's financial adversities is to anticipate problems and take action, before it's too late.

Be prepared to take action. Business conditions will likely deteriorate in 1991. Be prepared to respond quickly at the first sign of a slump by examining the effects of a slowdown on your business and outlining action that should be taken under various possible slowdown scenarios.

Recognize early warning signs. Don't wait for sales to slow down before taking action. Identify key indicators relevant to your business, which will point to deteriorating or improving business conditions, so you can take action at the earliest possible time. Critical indicators vary from business to business. Sudden changes in assets, such as accounts receivable or inventories—or decline in their turnover rates—these may indicate impending problems. On the liability side, rising trade payables or short-term debt often signal trouble ahead. Using debt, even short-term borrowings, to support the day-to-day operations of the business is usually a bad sign, unless the business is seasonal. The inability to pass along increased costs to your customers suggests that demand is weakening, often an outcome of a recession, or stronger competition. Either way, your company is likely to suffer a subsequent decline in sales.

Don't postpone taking corrective action. Once you have determined that problems may crop up, take action immediately to address them. Business owners are an optimistic lot, and they may delude themselves into thinking the problems will go away. You can bet they won't, particularly during tough economic times. There are a number of things you can do to help weather a slowdown in your business.

1. If your business has inventory, reducing inventories is often one of the best ways to cope with slowing business conditions. Not only does a lower inventory tie up less cash, it can also free up business credit lines, which can be used for other purposes if necessary.

2. Improving the management of accounts receivable is also an important means of keeping a business afloat. During a slowdown, your receivables will slow just like everyone else's, so you have to step up collection efforts. If you're facing particularly tight times, this is no time to mollycoddle your customers. They will simply take advantage of you. On the other side of the balance sheet, avoid paying your accounts payable early, but don't stretch out payables too long either. While delaying bill payments can help short-term cash flow, it will only aggravate the situation later on and could damage credit relationships. If extended payment terms can be arranged with some suppliers who may be anxious to prop up sales themselves, take advantage of them.

3. Loans should, of course, be kept to a minimum during a slowdown. Highly leveraged companies, whether they are multibillion-dollar corporations or small businesses, are likely to falter, if not fail, during this recession. If you get to the point where you are

having difficulty meeting your loan obligations, much of the advice concerning consumer credit problems contained in Chapter Twenty-one also applies to business indebtedness. Perhaps most important is keeping the bank informed of your problems and your plans to alleviate them.

4. If you haven't already, there probably are a number of areas where you can reduce expenses, particularly overhead, without adversely affecting your ability to do business. Approach layoffs with caution, unless you expect a lengthy slowdown. Layoffs often impair the quality of the services or products you are providing, not to mention the adverse effect on the morale of other employees. But if layoffs are necessary for the survival of the business, you have no choice.

5. If you are contemplating any major purchases for the business, you should consider whether it makes more sense to postpone them until you get a handle on how the recession ultimately will affect your business. On the other hand, you may find that, as larger companies curtail some of their products or services in response to the recession, you may have the opportunity to make inroads in other markets. This opportunity could justify some additional investment, as long as the new product or service is not far afield from your basic line of business.

6. No matter how bad the situation gets, try to avoid becoming preoccupied with the survival of your business, lest it take crucial time away from the management of day-to-day operations. Build your employees into a team that is dedicated to fighting and conquering the adverse effects of the slowdown. You'll probably be pleasantly surprised at the extra effort they are willing to give.

Separating Business Finances from
Personal Finances

As mentioned earlier, the biggest risk that the small business owner must confront in the face of deteriorating business conditions is not that you will lose the business, it is that in losing the business, you also will wipe out your personal resources. If the prospects for your business are very bleak during 1991, you may have to make a very difficult decision—whether you should pour more personal resources into the business and/or cosign more loans to the business, assuming you can get the loans at all, or whether you should cut your losses now. It is extremely difficult for most business owners to be objective and realistic about these matters. Only you can make that decision, but weigh carefully any action that could jeopardize your personal resources. It may not be worth it in the long run.

If you go through a business failure, remember that all is not lost. If you created a business once before, the odds are heavily in your favor that you can do it again. If you've had it with business ownership, take heart in the fact that many large companies find former business owners to be superb employees, because they are highly motivated and have qualities that are lacking in many employees of large companies—the ability to think innovatively and address problems effectively. I have a good friend who was victimized by the recession of the early 1980s. He had built up a large service business over the previous ten years, which collapsed in a matter of months. It wiped out all of his personal assets, including his home. Fortunately, he was blessed with a very supportive wife and children. After working for a company for about five years, and doing very well, he had the itch to strike out on his own again. He is now in the same line of business, but his organization is much leaner in size than his former, failed organization. I asked him how frightened he was of the recession of 1991. He said that it didn't bother him a bit. His company is lean, and although business has slowed down, he now knows what it takes to keep his business going in slow times because, as he says, "I learned from all the mistakes I made a decade ago." Moreover, he now owns his home free and clear, and has enough money in the bank to support the business for several years. His story is not at all unusual.

HOW SMALL BUSINESS OWNERS CAN SURVIVE THE RECESSION

- ☐ Be prepared to respond quickly, at the first sign of a slump in business.
- ☐ Identify and monitor key indicators that will provide early warning signals of impending problems.
- ☐ Take appropriate corrective action immediately, if and when problems arise.
- ☐ Avoid becoming preoccupied with the survival of the business at the expense of management of day-to-day operations.
- ☐ Evaluate thoroughly and realistically the wisdom of committing additional personal resources to the business. You don't want to jeopardize personal investments and credit if the survival of the business is seriously in question.

THE PSYCHOLOGICAL SIDE OF MONEY PROBLEMS

There's been a lot of arguing around the house lately. I mean, it's normal to argue, but not as much as we are. Things have really been tough for the last year. I finally got another job after being out of work for six months. We didn't lose the house, but we are so far behind on our bills that any time anyone in the family mentions anything about money, the fur starts to fly. I even yelled at my son yesterday when he asked for some money so that he could go out with his friends for dinner.

Everyone experiences money problems sometime during their lives, and everyone argues with family members about money matters, but that's of little comfort if your family is going through financial problems now.

Communication Is the Key

Sadly, money is so important to our self-esteem in this country, that money problems, even temporary money problems, can be devastating to us. For example, some people who have lost their jobs are afraid to tell anyone; they leave the house each morning as if they were going to work and return home in the evening. These same people probably aren't going to the unemployment office during their daily sojourns, because pride won't allow them to accept what they are entitled to, and probably need.

When confronted with money problems, we tend to withdraw at a time when we should be asking for help. We often spend too much time worrying about our problems and too little time working to address and resolve them. If there is one positive thing to say about financial problems, it is that they can be resolved. It may require a lot of work, it will probably require a lot of sacrifice, and it may well take a long time, but they can be resolved. But one other thing is for certain: They won't be resolved as easily as they might be if you don't share your problems with others, including family members.

It all boils down to communication. Good communication is important to your financial health, not just with family members and close friends, but also with people who can help you with your financial problems. For example, Chapter Twenty-two discusses what you should do if you fall behind, or think you'll fall behind in your mortgage. The answer? *Communicate* with the lender. Similarly, Chapter Twenty-one deals with coping with anxious creditors and using credit counselors. The solution is not to avoid creditors' calls and letters. Instead, you need to *communicate* with them openly and honestly. Creditors have a vested interest in helping you resolve your credit problems, and they are particularly well prepared to assist you during the current recession, because you're not alone in your problems. But, oh, does pride get in the way! It's not easy to get on the phone soon after you have been laid off to tell your friends and professional colleagues that you are in the market for a new job. How do you think they'll react? Is it really that embarrassing? If a friend or colleague called you to tell you the same thing, how would you react? When adversity strikes, don't let pride get in the way of good sense. Use the many resources available to you.

The Best of Times, the Worst of Times: You, Money Problems, and Your Family and Friends

Families survive financial crises. You've probably heard your parents or grandparents talk about the Great Depression. Families survived then. If you're going through your own great depression, you'll survive. It's as important to communicate openly with family members or close friends as it is with creditors, although you may feel that it is easier talking with creditors about your problems than it is family members. Generally, family members should share in any sacrifices that will be necessary to resolve the problem. Even if there is no immediate crisis, but you want to prepare for that eventuality during the recession, involve other family members in the planning and actions that must be taken. A spirit of cooperation will go a long way toward minimizing the family stress that inevitably accompanies a financial crisis. If your money problems seem to be causing you or your family too much stress—and they may—by all means consult with a mental-health professional.

When Your Financial Life Returns to Normal

If you want to start an argument with your spouse, money is the easiest excuse. You probably can find some money matter to complain about in less than ten seconds. So when your money problems are resolved, and your outlook is rosy once again, you'll still argue with your spouse or other loved ones over money. It seems that the only married couples who have never had an argument over money are those who are on their way to their own wedding receptions. But money disputes are not necessarily indicative of deeper problems. Actually, the vast majority of couples agree on important family financial matters, such as buying a home, educating the kids, and preparing for a comfortable retirement. Your disagreements tend to be over smaller day-to-day financial matters. There are a couple of easy things you can do to minimize inter-spousal money tensions. First, set aside one day every year to sit down with your spouse, review your financial status, and make some plans for next year. The date you select shouldn't be around tax-return preparation time, however. That's already stressful enough. Second, write down some realistic financial goals that you both want to accomplish over the next few years. What this all boils down to, of course, is improved communication with your spouse. Lack of communication about family finances, or for that matter, about any aspect of marriage, is a recipe for strife. But don't expect the arguments to go away entirely; because chances are you and your spouse will always have somewhat different approaches toward family money management. In fact, if you think about it, spenders tend to marry savers. While these couples may never eliminate marital money strife completely, they can, with a little communication, turn these warring extremes into a happy median.

MINIMIZING THE PSYCHOLOGICAL IMPACT OF MONEY PROBLEMS

☐ Seek the assistance and support of family members and friends if and when you experience financial problems. Resist the temptation to withhold this information from them.

☐ At the first sign of credit problems, contact your lenders so that you can work out a plan to repay the debt. Most lenders are prepared to work with you.

☐ Involve family members in developing and implementing plans to resolve financial problems.

☐ When your personal financial life returns to normal, remember that conflict with other family members or loved ones about family financial matters is inevitable, and is not usually indicative of deeper problems.

BANKRUPTCY—THE LAST RESORT

Since my husband got laid off, we've had a lot of trouble paying our bills. Even the credit counselor can't work out a repayment schedule that our creditors can accept. I'm afraid we're going to have to declare bankruptcy, but I'm not sure what that entails. Will we lose everything?

Personal bankruptcies are already on the rise, and as this recession gets worse, personal bankruptcy declarations may become more common. If you anticipate credit problems, work with a counselor, and take all the steps described in Chapter Twenty-one to pull yourself into solvency. Consider bankruptcy only as a last resort. But when all else has failed, it may be your only alternative. A bankruptcy stays on your credit history and makes it very hard to get credit for up to ten years. Of course, right now you probably hope you never see a credit card for the rest of your life, but odds are you'll feel differently in a few years.

On the bright side, declaring bankruptcy can get most of your debt problems solved, and will halt any legal actions that lenders may have taken against you.

Bankruptcy is a legal proceeding during which your responsibility for repaying certain debts is temporarily suspended while you and a bankruptcy trustee devise a plan for meeting as many of your credit obligations as possible. Your liability for certain debts may be limited to less than you owe, and other debts may be eliminated altogether. Once a plan has been worked out, you repay your debts from the forced sale of your assets or from your current income, according to the plan.

If you are considering filing for bankruptcy, it is extremely advisable that you consult with a lawyer. Obviously, this isn't a great time to incur additional expenses, but you can seek inexpensive legal assistance, and many lawyers are willing to work on a deferred compensation basis if they will be paid from the proceeds of a Chapter Seven bankruptcy, which is explained below.

Lawyers who specialize in bankruptcy may be inclined to push you to file, as an easy way out of your problems. Bankruptcy is not an easy way out, and should not be taken lightly. On the other hand, supposedly nonpartisan consumer credit counselors are generally supported by lending institutions and may discourage you from filing for bankruptcy even when it is your best option. Bankruptcy is major financial surgery. You wouldn't undertake major surgery without getting a second opinion—so get a second legal opinion before filing for bankruptcy.

Types of Bankruptcy Proceedings

There are basically two kinds of bankruptcy proceedings available to you: Chapter Seven, "straight bankruptcy," and Chapter Thirteen, the "wage-earner plan." The type you choose will depend on your income, the type of property you own, and the kind of debts you have.

Chapter Seven. If you file for bankruptcy under Chapter Seven, your debts will be eliminated by a liquidation of your assets. Some of your property will be exempted. A debtor can only file for Chapter Seven bankruptcy once every six years.

Chapter Thirteen. You must have continuous income from a job or other sources to file for Chapter Thirteen, and your indebtedness must be below certain limits. Bankruptcy under Chapter Thirteen generally carries less stigma than bankruptcy under Chapter Seven. Under Chapter Thirteen, the debtor works out a plan for the repayment of outstanding debts under the supervision of a referee and the federal bankruptcy court. The repayment generally takes three years, after which any remaining debt is forgiven. In effect, this keeps creditors from getting at your assets and allows you to keep enough current income to meet living expenses during the time you're working off the debt. You must adhere to a strict budget, and all of your excess earnings must be devoted to paying off debts. If need be, a debtor can file a new Chapter Thirteen proceeding as soon as he or she has completed payment on a prior Chapter Thirteen proceeding. There is no limit to the number of times you can file, but the courts can deny the filing if they believe it is being abused. Chapter Thirteen can be used to avoid a car repossession or mortgage foreclosure. Also, some debts that are not forgivable under Chapter Seven, such as old student loans and old tax obligations, are forgivable under Chapter Thirteen, if the court rules that they would constitute an excessive burden for the debtor.

What's Protected from Bankruptcy

You will not lose everything you own during bankruptcy proceedings, and debtors' jails have been abolished. If your debts are within certain limits and you have a steady job, you may be able to avert a forced sale altogether, by filing Chapter Thirteen.

If you are forced to file Chapter Seven, you will be able to exempt certain assets from the sale. Exactly how much you will be able to exempt depends on what you own and whether you file under federal or state law, but at the least, you will be allowed a $7,500 exemption, which can be applied toward your home, land, motor vehicle, burial plot, business inventory, or other real estate or personal property, over and above mortgages and liens on the property. In addition, the debtor may exempt:

- up to $1,200 in one motor vehicle;
- up to $4,000 of household goods—up to $200 per debtor, per item;
- up to $500 of personal jewelry;
- up to $750 of professional books and tools of your trade;
- any term life insurance and whole life insurance up to a cash value of $4,000;
- an unlimited amount of professionally prescribed health aids for the debtor or dependents;
- Social Security, unemployment, welfare, disability, illness and retirement benefits, except under special circumstances;
- certain types of injury or loss payments up to set limits;
- up to $400 of any property (called the "wild card" exemption).

Other rules also apply to exempt assets. Your attorney will explain them to you.

What Debts Won't Be Cleared by the Proceedings

Under Chapter Thirteen, you will have to work off all your debts. If you file for Chapter Seven, on the other hand, most of your creditors will be forced to accept their portion of the proceeds from the forced sale of your assets as payment in full, even if they receive only a portion of the amount you owe. However, there are certain debts that you will still have to pay under Chapter Seven.

- Certain back taxes or any fraudulent taxes
- Credit card charges incurred within forty days of filing. Do not make credit card purchases if you are filing for bankruptcy. If you do, you may be accused of fraud.
- Personal loans and installment purchases made within forty days of filing
- Alimony
- Child-support payments
- Student loans, subject to certain restrictions
- Any debts you inadvertently omit from your filing
- Money owed someone for intentional harm done them
- Automobile accident claims in which you were drunk or reckless or other traffic tickets or fines from violating the law in criminal cases
- Debts resulting from fraud or false financial statements, unless the lender told you to make those statements
- Any assets converted to exempt assets within ninety days of filing may be challenged by the lender or bankruptcy trustee.

Emerging from Bankruptcy

Some lenders will be willing to grant a loan to a family or individual who has declared bankruptcy in the past, particularly if the bankruptcy was caused by factors beyond their control. However, it can still be very difficult for an ex-bankrupt to obtain the kind of credit that previously supported his or her lifestyle. The type of bankruptcy you file may affect your future credit prospects as well. If you filed Chapter Seven, creditors may be reassured by the fact that you are prohibited from filing again for six years. If you filed Chapter Thirteen and paid back a major portion of your debts, potential lenders may be willing to take a chance on you. However, you should recognize that many people are forced to reduce their standard of living for quite some time after declaring bankruptcy. Whatever your situation, whatever the forces that compelled you to declare bankruptcy, the worst is over, and you will be able to emerge and begin anew. Rebuilding your credit will take time and perseverance. While the number of bankruptcies has been increasing as the economy has slipped into recession, a lender will still be reticent to take a chance on you, at first. The best way to do so is gradually to rebuild your banking relationships, so you can demonstrate your creditworthiness.

IF YOU ARE CONSIDERING FILING FOR BANKRUPTCY TO END YOUR CREDIT PROBLEMS

- ☐ Try to work something out to avoid filing for bankruptcy. (See Chapter Twenty-one.)
- ☐ Consult with a credit counselor and an attorney.
- ☐ Familiarize yourself with the two types of bankruptcy proceedings, and decide in conjunction with an attorney which one would be more advantageous to you.
- ☐ Determine whether enough of your debts would be discharged by bankruptcy proceedings to make it worthwhile.

☐ Determine how you will use your property exemptions.

☐ Work with a credit counselor to devise a plan to pay the debts that will not be discharged through the proceedings.

☐ Work hard to rebuild your creditworthiness when you emerge so that you won't repeat your credit problems.

IF INFLATION HEATS UP

I always thought that recessions meant prices would moderate, but now I am reading that the inflation rate is increasing. Does this mean we're going to get a slowdown in business, lots of unemployment, with rising prices to boot? They say life is unfair, but how unfair can it get?

Simultaneous recession and inflation is not unheard of. It happened in 1973–1974 and again in 1981. Business was down, stock prices were declining, and prices of consumer goods soared. As of late 1990, more than a few economists were expressing an opinion that inflation may well heat up in 1991. The consumer price index rose at a near-double-digit annual rate in August and September 1990. Some other measures also pointed toward higher inflation, although higher inflation is far from a certainty. This chapter will highlight some tips that may help you if and when the inflation rate rises well above the current 5 to 6 percent range and is expected to persist.

- If a period of higher inflation is likely, you should account for those costs in your budgeting, and make the necessary changes in your spending to reflect increased costs. While wages typically rise with inflation, there is always a lag between rising costs and rising income, which is going to have to be made up somewhere.

- If prices rise, so must your savings, because you will need more money set aside to meet the higher costs of whatever you will use your savings for, including coping with family financial emergencies and accumulating enough resources to be able to retire comfortably.

- Review your insurance coverage limits in light of higher inflation, particularly your homeowner's or renter's insurance policies. While some insurance companies automatically increase the limits of coverage each year to bring the protection into line with current costs, many do not, and even those who do may not increase the limits sufficiently to account for higher inflation. This applies both to your home and to your personal possessions. Valuables, in particular, may increase significantly during a period of high inflation.

- If you find that consumer goods costs are increasing rapidly, as they did in the early 1980s, consider buying household necessities in bulk. But don't go overboard and spend money you may need to help you through the recession.

- You will hear a lot of people say that borrowing is a good thing to do during a period of high inflation, because you can repay these loans with "cheaper dollars." Many families have been ruined financially by taking that advice during earlier inflationary periods. The catch? They borrowed for silly reasons and didn't have any "cheaper dollars" around to repay their loans.

- If you have an adjustable-rate mortgage, and you expect that inflation will heat up and continue indefinitely, it may be time to switch to a fixed-rate mortgage. Check the provisions of your adjustable rate mortgage to see how high the interest rate can go. While you may not be able to lock in a very attractive rate on a fixed-rate mortgage now, it may be better than having to suffer from an even higher rate on your adjustable mortgage.

- Inflation is a tremendous problem to any retiree whose income is wholly or partially fixed. Social Security benefits rise with the cost of living, but most pensions and annuities are fixed. Hence, retirees should have at least a portion of their personal retirement funds in investments that offer some hedge against inflation. Retirees also should save some of their income well into their old age so that they will be able to cope with periodic high inflation. See Chapter Twenty-five for additional advice for retirees on coping with the uncertain economy.

- When inflation is soaring, stock investments can, but don't always, perform well. So-called hard assets, such as housing, real estate, and precious metals, tend to do well in times of rapid inflation, but this is not always the case either. Long-term fixed-income investments do rather poorly during an inflationary period because inflation pushes up interest rates, so the value of older bonds with lower coupons sinks, sometimes dramatically. A safe harbor during periods of high inflation is short-term cash-equivalent investments, whose interest rates tend to rise as inflation rises. Once interest rates get quite high, you can lock in the attractive yields by buying longer-term bonds. It's hard to know when inflation is at its peak, so you probably should hedge your bets by laddering the maturities on your fixed-income investments. See Chapter Fourteen.

- Since real estate generally has been a good inflation hedge, your home becomes an even more

attractive investment during a period of high inflation, and you could well profit from home improvements.

- In periods of high inflation, money invested in
stocks and other property is not as likely to lose
its purchasing power as money that simply is set
aside in fixed-income securities that have a fixed
dollar value. Of course, stocks do not provide a
guaranteed hedge against inflation. There is simply
no close connection between inflationary or defla-
tionary conditions and the movement of stock
prices. *Note:* Many experts advise against purchasing utility stocks during a period of threatened
or actual inflation, because utilities have a great
deal of trouble performing well in an environment
where their debt costs are rising due to higher
interest rates, but these higher costs are hard to
pass on to customers because of regulations.

- Don't fall for the hard-sell tactics that may be
leveled at you by salespeople intent on protecting
your home and hearth against the ravages of inflation. They want to sell you guaranteed inflation
hedges, such as rare coins, gemstones, and gold
bullion. The only guarantee in these offers is that
you are going to be taken, if you take them up on
their offer.

PLANNING FOR A
SECURE FINANCIAL
FUTURE

30

"BEEN DOWN SO LONG"— GETTING BACK ON YOUR FEET

This recession set us back a bit. We had to dip into our savings, and the bills mounted, but we're looking forward to getting back to where we were. Then, we'll begin to improve our personal finances so that we will be better prepared for the future.

Recessions do end. When we're going through them, however, we wonder if they ever will. We may be in for a slow recovery after this recession, so don't be surprised if there is some uncertainty as to what the postrecession economy will be like.

Once the economy starts to turn around, you should evaluate where you stand financially and begin to plan for better times ahead. Millions of people will have been hurt by this recession through unemployment, bad investment decisions, or bad investment performance, or other problems in making ends meet. Some may have had years', if not a lifetime's worth of savings wiped out. Most of those who went into the recession loaded with debt will undoubtedly emerge from the recession loaded with debt. Whatever your circumstances, you can begin to rebuild so that you will be able to look forward to a more secure financial future.

The following list will help you take action to get back on your feet.

1. **Review your debt situation.** You may have been preoccupied with your tenuous loan situation during the recession, and now that matters have settled down, you probably would like to forget about them. That's not possible, of course, but at least your finances may have stablized sufficiently to begin making progress on getting your loan balances reduced. This should be a high-priority item as you emerge from the recession. By all means, don't let the postrecession euphoria motivate you to add to your loan balances if they already were causing you problems.

2. **Improve your credit standing.** Because so many millions of families went into this recession with too much debt, many will emerge with impaired credit ratings. If this applies to you, you should make an extra effort to assure that you reestablish your good credit standing as soon as possible—not so you can borrow yourself into trouble again, but rather to restore your ability to borrow, in the event you need to in the future for worthwhile purposes or to meet financial emergencies.

3. **Restore your emergency fund.** If you, like many people, had to dip into your emergency fund to make ends meet during the economic downturn, restore it to a level of at least three months' living expenses as soon as possible. If you didn't have an emergency fund in the first place, you may have seen how important it was as you struggled through the recession. Since your financial situation should be improving somewhat, you can now focus in on building up your emergency fund. I hope that by now you know what is required to save the money necessary to accumulate a

financial cushion. Quite simply, you must learn to live beneath your means.

4. **Evaluate postponed expenses.** The financial strain of the recession may have caused you to postpone some necessary household expenses. If your financial situation has improved, review these items to see if it would be prudent to incur these expenses now. For example, if you postponed needed car repairs, home repairs, or appliance replacements, you may decide that now is the time to make the repairs or purchase the appliances.

5. **Be realistic.** Getting back on your feet won't happen overnight. This is one of the frustrating things about personal finance. We can get into financial trouble in a matter of weeks or months, but it takes a lot longer to recover. Don't let financial recovery get you down. If you can make progress each day, whether it involves foregoing an expense that can be forgone, looking for ways to improve your job performance or earn outside income, or by putting a few dollars in a savings account, you *are* on the road to recovery. And that progress, however small it might seem, will snowball.

6. **Don't revert to your old habits.** Unfortunately, many people who have been adversely affected by the recession will struggle to get on their feet, only to revert back to their old habits. Sadly, many people in this country are consigned to a lifetime of living hand-to-mouth. I am not talking about the impoverished, I am talking about middle-income, and even high-income individuals and families. You know what your past financial experience has been. Do you really want to go back to your old ways, or is it time to make some progress so that you don't have to live in constant fear of creditors, or illness, or whatever other conditions might befall you? Do you really want to have to work the rest of your life? Believe me, it really doesn't take

that much effort to change your lifestyle so that you can turn the corner. You know that you should change, and there is no better time than now to begin to manage your finances more sensibly.

7. **Treat yourself to something nice.** You've probably been through a lot during the recession. Times were tough, family relationships were strained, and you frequently wondered whether you would survive. Well, you did, and I think that you should reward yourself and your loved ones by doing something that contradicts just about everything that I've asked you to do in this book. Go out and splurge. Take them to the most expensive restaurant in town—it probably could use the business after the recession—or spend a weekend at an expensive resort. Just don't put it on your credit card. Why do I suggest that you do something so financially frivolous? Because you survived the tough times. You deserve a treat.

PROFITING FROM PROSPERITY

This book has covered a variety of topics, ranging from the unpleasant to the downright depressing. Tough times are tough on people. If you have had to suffer during the bad times, you certainly deserve to prosper during the good times. A few tips that may help you on your way to well-deserved prosperity follow.

1. **Readjust your investments to reflect new market conditions.** The investment strategies that were outlined in Part III of the book emphasized defensive investing. As the economy begins to improve, you will want to readjust your investments away from a defensive strategy to a more aggressive strategy. Be bold, but be prudent. For example, you may want to increase the proportion of your investments invested in stocks above that suggested in Chapter Eleven. The outlook for real estate may improve, so you might consider real estate investments as well.

2. **Tune into new opportunities.** You probably spent a lot of time worrying about the recession. Since you don't have to spend your time worrying about a recession now—at least until the next recession comes along—spend that time looking for ways to profit from rapidly evolving trends and world conditions. Some

things that come to mind include our aging population, environmental concerns, the opening up of world markets, and further technological advances of yet unknown proportions.

3. **Look for opportunities to advance in your career.** Perhaps you lost your job during the recession and took another one that is far from ideal. As the economy begins to pick up steam, you may find that an opportunity will open up for a better job. If you are happy where you are, begin to plan how you will advance at your place of work. The single best way to improve your financial situation is to have a steadily rising income that exceeds the rate of inflation. So if you can advance in your career, and thereby earn more income while keeping your expenses under control, you'll be in fat city.

4. **Participate in retirement plans.** As most Americans struggled through the recession, retirement planning took a back seat. Our attention was focused on more pressing matters. But preparing for retirement is one of the most crucial tasks for all working-age people. Now that you are back on a firmer financial footing, review where you stand with respect to accumulating resources for retirement. Unless you expect to receive a seven-figure inheritance or are fortunate enough to marry someone with a seven-figure trust, you should be participating to the maximum in any company-sponsored retirement plans, such as 401(k) plans. Consider contributing to an IRA each year, as well. If you are self-employed or if you have income from moonlighting, you also should set up a self-employed retirement arrangement, such as a Keogh or a simplified employee pension (SEP) plan. Whether you are an employee or are self-employed, neglecting to participate in these tax-deferred plans is likely to delay your retirement, if you will be able to afford to retire at all.

5. **Prepare for the next recession.** If you conduct your financial life as if the next recession is just around the corner, someday you will be correct, and you will be well prepared for it. There are a variety of things you should do in your day-to-day life, when times aren't so difficult, to improve your financial well-being when times get tough again.

- Organize your records and set plans for the future
- Prepare budgets
- Spend wisely
- Maintain adequate and comprehensive insurance coverage
- Maintain your good credit and only borrow for worthwhile purposes
- Save regularly
- Invest wisely
- Assure a comfortable retirement by participating in retirement-savings plans

We've come a long way. My greatest hope is that you will begin to take *some* action to help you through the current recession, so you can take advantage of the prosperity that will inevitably follow. Do take some action. You'll like the feeling, and pretty soon you'll not only be recession-proof, but also, more importantly, you'll be well on your way to achieving financial peace of mind. Good luck!

APPENDIX:
WHAT THE NEW TAX LAW
MEANS TO YOU

As if the sour economy weren't enough, they've passed the biggest single tax increase in history. I've heard people say that the two things in life you can't avoid are death and taxes—but at least death doesn't get worse every time Congress convenes. I'm working all my waking hours to keep a roof over my family and food on the table. How am I going to find time to figure out what these new taxes are all about?

The new tax bill is officially known as the Revenue Reconciliation Act of 1990. The bad news is that it raises taxes for a lot of taxpayers; if not on their income, then on the pleasures of life like alcohol, tobacco, yachts, and Lear Jets. The good news is that we're not going to have to spend time and money figuring out how to beat the new rules, since there isn't much anyone can do to avoid the tax increases. Maybe Congress recognized that we already have enough to worry about in 1991, without having to find ways to beat the new tax rules. The tax drafters may have finally devised an almost loopholeless set of tax rules. There will be some strategies you can use to save taxes under the new rules, but the savings are more likely to be a few dollars rather than a few thousand dollars.

Nothing in the new tax law should cause you to make any basic changes in the way you handle your personal finances and investments. Nevertheless, you should become familiar with how the provisions affect you, since you may find your tax bill raised or lowered somewhat in 1991. A description of the major provisions of the new tax law, below, is followed by a section showing how the rules may affect you. Most of the changes in the new tax law begin to take effect in 1991. Don't be surprised if more revenue enhancing tax legislation is enacted in 1991 or 1992.

What Changes Our Congress Hath Wrought

Income tax rates increased. The newly established 31 percent marginal tax brackets will be adjusted for inflation in subsequent years and begin at the following amounts in 1991.

Single individual	$49,200
Joint return	$82,050
Head of household	$70,350
Married filing separately	$14,025
Estates and trusts	$10,350

Capital gains taxes modified. The maximum capital gains tax rate is 28 percent. For taxpayers in the 15 percent bracket, capital gains will be taxed at 15 percent, except for that portion of the capital gain, if any, that pushes their income into the 28 percent bracket.

Alternative minimum tax increased. The alternative minimum tax (AMT) rate is raised to 24 percent from 21 percent.

Personal exemptions for high-income taxpayers reduced. The deduction for personal exemptions is reduced or even eliminated for certain high-income taxpayers. If the taxpayer's adjusted gross income exceeds the following threshold amounts, the deduction for exemptions is reduced by 2 percent for each $2,500 ($1,250 if married and filing separately) or fraction thereof by which adjusted gross income exceeds that amount.

Single individual	$100,000
Joint return	$150,000
Head of household	$125,000
Married, filing separately	$75,000

Itemized deductions for high-income taxpayers reduced. An individual whose adjusted gross income exceeds $100,000 ($50,000 for married persons filing separately) in 1991 (adjusted for inflation in subsequent years) is required to reduce itemized deductions by 3 percent of the excess over that threshold. In no event, however, may the reduction be more than 80 percent of allowable itemized deductions, not counting the deductions for medical expenses, investment interest, or casualty losses.

Unnecessary cosmetic surgery is no longer a deductible medical expense.

Earned income credit increased. The percentages of income for determining the amount of the basic earned income credit are increased over a four-year transitional period. A higher percentage applies if there are two or more qualifying children. The credit is expanded to include a new supplemental credit for health insurance premiums and for taxpayers with a qualifying child under the age of one.

Excise taxes increased. The gasoline tax is increased from nine to fourteen cents a gallon. Excise taxes are also increased for alcoholic beverages, tobacco products, and luxury goods.

Other provisions:
- State and local employees who are not covered by public pensions must pay Social Security payroll taxes.
- Tax credits through 1991 for research and development, low-income housing, and others are extended.
- The exclusion for employer-provided educational assistance benefits is extended through 1991, as is the exclusion for employer-provided group legal services.
- Taxpayer identification numbers must be provided for any dependents who have attained age one as of the close of the tax year, effective after 1990.
- The cap on wages and self-employment income considered in calculating the 1.45 percent Medicare hospital insurance payroll tax has been increased to $125,000.

Figuring Out How the New Tax Rules Affect You

Total tax bill. If you earn an income under $100,000, the new tax rules will probably have little, if any, effect on your income tax bill. Wealthier people will see their taxes rise. The marginal tax rate (the tax rate on each additional dollar earned) on high-income people increases from 28 percent to 31 percent. But the phaseout of some personal exemptions and tax deductions creates "backdoor" taxes, which can raise the marginal rate to as much as 34 percent.

Capital gains. The capital gains rate is little changed under the new rules, so you probably should not change your investment strategies. But be prepared to be besieged by brokers, insurance agents, and others selling investments that purportedly take advantage of the new tax rules. Instead of falling for these pitches, base your investment decisions on the merits of the investment, not just the tax benefits.

Tax-advantaged investments. Retirement investment plans will become more valuable for any working-age taxpayers whose tax rates increase under the new regulations. The higher your tax bracket, the greater the investment income you can earn by placing investments in a tax-deferred retirement plan, such as an IRA, 401(k) plan, or Keogh plan.

Marriage penalty. If people got married for financial reasons alone, the new tax law would certainly discourage them. The way the new tax brackets are structured increases the "marriage penalty." The larger your income, the more your marriage will cost you. For example, a couple with a combined income of $150,000 and average deductions will pay about $1,800 more tax if they were married than if they're single.

Illustrations. The following illustrations, which are based on studies conducted by major accounting firms, show the impact of the new tax rules on various hypothetical income and family situations. Note that the increased levies on gasoline, alcohol, and tobacco affect everyone, but the added costs are relatively small for most people.

- A couple with two children and an income of $40,000 would have no change in their taxes as a result of the new rules.
- A family of four with income of $115,000 would have a $400 decrease in income taxes, because their marginal rate falls from 33 percent to 31

percent, but they would use about $300 of that savings to pay the higher Medicare payroll tax.

- A widow with an income of $60,000 would have almost no change in income taxes as a result of the new rules.
- The very high-income taxpayer incurs higher taxes under the Revenue Reconciliation Act of 1990, but not very much higher. A couple with an income of $1,100,000 would see their tax bill rise about 10 percent, from $187,000 to $206,000. They will find it virtually impossible to avoid the higher tax burden, but they probably can afford to pay the increased taxes anyway.

TO FIND OUT HOW THE NEW TAX RULES AFFECT YOU

☐ Although you can't do much, if anything, to lower your taxes under the new law, you should still become familiar with whether and how its provisions affect you.

☐ If you have a low or moderate income, the new tax rules will have little or no effect on your taxes. However, higher excise taxes for certain items, like gasoline and alcohol, could increase your living expenses.

☐ If you have a high income, you should project how the new rules will affect you in 1991. Most high-income taxpayers will pay more, and should plan for it now. Be particularly careful about how the higher alternative minimum tax might affect you.

☐ The new tax laws probably won't require you to change how you invest, except that tax-deferred retirement savings plans may be more advantageous for certain taxpayers.

☐ Keep abreast of any future changes in the tax laws. Congress is not finished with us yet.